Summarised History of the English Language – Who, What, Where, When and How

Author: Shayne T Pattie. Editor: Charmaine Hawthorn.
Cover Illustrator: Angela Pattie

Contents

Why This Book 6

Defining the term 'English Language' 9

Influences and Origins of the English Language 16

    Key War Influences 23

    Key Religious Influences 25

    Media Technological Influences 27

    Memes and Emojis 34

    Other Technology Influences 37

    Key Spoken Art, Written Art and Author influences 42

    Conlang Influences 46

    Other Key People and their Influences 53

    Industry Specific Jargon Influences 59

        Sailing 59

        Medical 60

        Legal 60

        Scientific 61

        Political / Diplomatic 61

        Military 62

        Computer Technologies 65

        Commerce 65

        Sports 66

        Entertainment 66

Fashion 67

Finance 67

Aviation 68

Construction and Architecture 68

Music 68

Artificial Intelligence 69

Old English – 450-1150CE 72

Pre-Old English 74

Germanic Influence 76

Old Norse, Latin and French 77

Old English Inflected Language and Grammar Rules
.... 82

Middle English – 1150-1500CE 94

Simplified English 94

Black Death 96

Norman French Influence Decline 97

Regional Dialect Diversity 98

Middle English Influences, Changes and Rules ... 100

Regional Dialect Diversity 110

Early Modern 1500-1700CE & Modern English 1700CE to Present 114

Early Modern English 116

The Great Vowel Shift 124

Grimm's & Verner's Laws 127

Jespersen's Cycle... 131

Pre-Printing Press Standardisation 133

Printing Press Influences on Outdated Sounds and Hypercorrections 135

Transition Away from Gendered Nouns 138

Classism ('Inkhorn') Social and Capitalist Influences 143

    Animals and Food.. 149

Math Influence on English................................. 153

Beginnings of American English Influence 155

English and its Modern Variants 156

    Kachru Three Circles Model 156

    Global Language 158

Modern English Nouns, Verbs & More..................... 166

    4 Major word classes 167

        Nouns... 167

        Verbs 167

        Adjectives 168

        Adverbs 168

    Other word classes 169

        Prepositions 169

        Pronouns 169

Determiners 169

Conjunctions 170

Interjections 170

Prefixes 170

Suffixes 171

Tenses 171

Acronyms 172

Paralinguistics 173

Particles 173

Grammatical Expletives 173

Neologisms and Functional Shifts 174

Pronunciation & Basic Rules in Modern English 175

Concluding – English the Ever-Changing Language. 187

References 193

Why This Book

Most modern languages share similarities with each other when alterations of the official language are included. This book will be focusing on my love of history and the history of the English language. This book aims to explore many of the various influences culturally, linguistically and other, that led to what we now know as the 'English Language'.

There are three tools for studying language historically Articulatory Phonetics representation of the sounds of a language), Sociolinguistics (how language operates in society) and Comparative Philology (reconstructing earlier forms of a language. This book will be focusing on aspects of all three with a stronger focus on the bidirectional societal influences on the development of the English language.

This book is aimed towards people interested in history and language and has been written for those who want to explore the content for personal learning or for basic educational purposes. It provides a great summary on the current and previous research into what makes the English language so interesting.

I have always been interested in human history and had long wondered why the English language made no logical sense (from what I had been taught). I was finally inspired to write this book after seeing the following image created by Minna Sundberg (Sundberg, M., 2015). Whilst there are many brilliant resources, I hope that this book provides an interesting summary that helps to spark the interest of others into the English language and its beginnings. I found that most resources, whilst great, went into too much detail for the casual learner, and my hope is that this book will spark enough interest that you, the reader will wish to pursue your own journey of learning about the English language. This book title begins with "Summarised" to help the reader understand that I have read and summarised a lot of the literature available in an attempt to make learning this topic easier.

Defining the term 'English Language'

In simple terms we call the language 'English' because of his historical association with England. However, the language itself is a lot more complex.

The term 'English language' can be defined as the West Germanic language of the Indo-European language family that originated in early medieval England and has evolved into a global lingua franca (a language that is adopted as a common language between speakers whose native languages are different) (Jenkins, J., & Baker, W., 2023). It can also be defined as the grammar and words a speaker knows and uses to construct English sentences (Chomsky, N., 1965).

Today English is still thought to be one of the more difficult languages to learn (depending on what your original language is) due largely in part to the contradictions and messy history that led to today's English language. Due to the many influences on the English language, relying on phonetics is often unreliable. British philologist William Walter Skeat reportedly said, that no one can tell how to pronounce an English word unless he has at some time or other heard it. Mispronunciations of complex words often suggest that a person learned them through reading rather than through spoken conversation (Read, A. W., 1978).

The modern English language at its core is still a West Germanic language because of the major influences on its development. However, as will be discussed in the book later, it has been influenced directly and indirectly by many different cultures and languages including, but not limited to – Old English, Old Norse, Latin variations, Norman French, French, Dutch, Flemish, Greek, Celtic dialects, Welsch dialects, Scottish and Gaelic dialects, Arabic, Hebrew, Sanskrit (indirectly) Italian, Spanish, Portuguese, Hindi and Urdu, Persian (indirectly), Turkish, Mandarin and Cantonese, Malay, Swahili, Aztec Nahuatl, Algonquian languages, West African languages and many more (Burchfield, R. (Ed.)., 1994).

Communication is never one directional, and although English is now the dominant language of the modern world, it is still evolving and continues to change based on multi-directional influences as it to, influences its environment. The previous experiences of explorers, scholars, artists and others who interacted with different cultures and languages demonstrate that the encounter with the "other" is not simply a matter of bringing in new words; it is the occasion for reflecting on the nature and history of language itself (Lerer, S., 2008).

The following poem was originally written in 1920 by Gerard Nolst Trenité (pen name Charivarius) known as "The Chaos" (Trenité, G. N., 1870–1946). It is a great example of why English is so difficult to speak and spell and is a great example of how the English language has been influenced by various events over time including cultures, war, technologies and others.

"Dearest creature in creation
Studying English pronunciation,
I will teach you in my verse
Sounds like corpse, corps, horse, and worse.

I will keep you, Susy, busy,
Make your head with heat grow dizzy;
Tear in eye, your dress will tear;
So shall I! Oh hear my prayer.

Just compare heart, beard and heard,
Dies and diet, lord and word,
Sword and sward, retain and Britain.

(Mind the latter, how it's written.)

*Now I surely will not plague you
With such words as plaque and ague.
But be careful how you speak:
Say break and steak, but bleak and streak.*

*Cloven, oven, how and low,
Script, receipt, show, poem and toe.*

*Hear me say, devoid of trickery,
Daughter, laughter and Terpsichore,
Typhoid, measles, topsails, aisles,
Exiles, similes and reviles;*

*Scholar, vicar, and cigar,
Solar, mica, war and far;*

*One, anemone, Balmoral,
Kitchen, lichen, laundry, laurel;*

*Gertrude, German, wind and mind,
Scene, Melpomene, mankind.*

*Billet does not rhyme with ballet,
Bouquet, wallet, mallet, chalet.
Blood and flood are not like food,
Nor is mould like should and would.*

*Viscous, viscount, load and broad,
Toward, to forward, to reward.
And your pronunciation's OK
When you correctly say croquet,*

*Rounded, wounded,
grieve and sieve,
Friend and fiend, alive
and live.*

*Ivy, privy, famous;
clamour
And enamour rhyme with
hammer.
River, rival, tomb, bomb,
comb,
Doll and roll and some
and home.*

*Stranger does not rhyme
with anger,
Neither does devour with
clangour.
Souls but foul, haunt but
aunt,
Font, front, wont, want,
grand, and grant.*

*Shoes, goes, does. Now
first say finger,
And then singer, ginger,
linger,*

*Real, zeal, mauve, gauze
and gauge,
Marriage, foliage,
mirage, and age.
Query does not rhyme
with very,
Nor does fury sound like
bury.*

*Dost, lost, post and doth,
cloth, loth.
Job, nob, bosom,
transom, oath.
Though the differences
seem little,
We say actual but
victual.*

*Refer does not rhyme
with defer.
Pfeffer does and zephyr,
heifer.
Mint, pint, senate and
sedate;
Dull, bull, and George ate
late.*

Scenic, Arabic, Pacific,
Science, conscience, scientific.

Liberty, library, heave and heaven,
Rachel, ache, moustache, eleven.
We say hallowed, but allowed,
People, leopard, towed and vowed.

Mark the differences, moreover,
Between mover, cover, clover;
Leeches, breeches, wise, precise,
Chalice, but police and lice;

Camel, constable, unstable,
Principle, disciple, label.

Petal, panel and canal,
Wait and bait, and mate and male.

Mince, pints, masculine, feminine,
Henry, penitence, and denizen.

Rhymed with wrong is rong, not wring,
Nor is pong the same as ping.

Say said, pay, paid, laid, but plaid.
Now once more: you prick your finger.

Say the close of all we've had:
It's enough to drive one mad!

So I take it you already know
Of tough and bough and cough and dough?

Some may stumble, but not you,
On hiccough, thorough, slough, and through.

Well done! And now you wish, perhaps,
To learn of less familiar traps?

Beware of heard, a dreadful word
That looks like beard and sounds like bird.
And dead: it's said like bed, not bead –
For goodness' sake, don't call it "deed"!

Watch out for meat and great and threat –
They rhyme with suite and straight and debt.

A moth is not a moth in mother
Nor both in bother, broth in brother.
And here is not a match for there
Nor dear and fear for bear and pear.

And then there's dose and rose and lose –
Just look them up – and goose and choose.

And cork and work and card and ward,
And font and front and word and sword,
And do and go and thwart and cart –
Come, come, I've hardly made a start!

A dreadful language? Man alive,
I'd mastered it when I was five!"

Influences and Origins of the English Language

There is a large gap between 50,000 years ago, when humans probably started using language, and the time from which we have historical evidence for language in the form of writing (Yule, G., 2022). The earliest evidence of written language includes Harappan/Indus Valley writing dates approximately 5,500 years ago, Egyptian approximately 5,300 years ago, and Mesopotamian cuneiform is over 5,100 years old, with historians suggesting that these civilisations may have had contact with each other. The Chinese characters date back approximately 3,500 years and Mesoamerican (Mayan) writing is approximately 2,500 years old. Ancient writings allow us to understand long-term linguistic change. Knowledge of earlier stages also gives rise to speculation about why language changes and what the original language is (Daniels, P. T., 2013).

Some research has suggested that the pre-writing language development and proto-writing systems influenced the development of other languages, including those that would eventually contribute to

English. Examples of this influence on the development of the Old English language include the adoption of runic symbols (futhorc) derived from earlier Mediterranean alphabets, numerical and record-keeping concepts traced to Mesopotamian tally systems, and mythological or cultural motifs passed down through oral traditions originating in proto-Indo-European societies. In this context, other research has also explored how cave art, tally stick communication, and early memory aids such as knotted cords (quipu-like devices) or carved mnemonic notches, helped influence language development through visual symbolism, the externalisation of memory, and the creation of shared cultural references that could be 'read' or interpreted by a community (Miyagawa, S., Lesure, C., & Nóbrega, V. A., 2018).

Sir William Jones, a British judge in late-eighteenth-century India, made the larger scholarly community aware of correspondences between Latin, Greek, and Sanskrit. These correspondences had been written about by others, such as Comenius and Scalinger in the 17th century, but weren't accepted until Jones' time. Jones' work made it possible for scholars such as Rask and Grimm to formulate sound laws and postulate what the predecessor of Latin and Greek might have been. Grimm's Law, for example, is one of the results of such work as is the grouping of certain languages into an Indo-European family (Jones, W., 1786).

The English language is thought to be descended from a common ancestor known as Proto-Germanic from around 500 BCE, and with a lot of linguistic analysis, it has been theorised that the Proto-Indo-European arose approximately six thousand years ago leading to the Proto-Germanic languages. English foundationally is still rooted in Germanic languages, however, depending on how far back we go, it has many direct and indirect influences (Hogg, R. M., 1992).

The Proto-Indo-European (PIE) language tree is theorised to be the historical foundation for subsequent languages eventually connecting to the English language. One (less accepted) theory suggests that the PIE language may have originated in India. However, the more widely accepted theory is that it arose from the Pontic–Caspian steppe near the Black Sea. This second, more accepted theory uses archaeological and genetic evidence such as migration patterns and Y-DNA haplogroups (migration of males) and the reconstructions of PIE vocabulary (e.g., words for temperate-climate plants, animals, wagons, horses) point to a homeland with those ecological conditions, matching the steppe environment (Saag, L., Laneman, M., Varul, L., Malve, M., Valk, H., et. al., 2019).

As well as the PIE lineage, a distinctly different language foundation known as the 'Uralic' root led to influences on languages such as Finnic languages (Finnish (Suomi), Estonian (Eesti) and Karelian), Ugric languages (Hungarian (Magyar), Khanty and Mansi) and Samoyedic languages (far north Siberia) (Nenets and Nganasan). Whilst the Uralic root isn't connected to the PIE lineage, the natural evolution of language through multidirectional cultural sharing, still indirectly influenced the development of the English language with words be borrowed and absorbed such as Sauna, Coach and Tundra (de Heer, M., Blokland, R., Dunn, M., & Vesakoski, O., 2024).

Returning to the PIE lineage, several different language groups began to emerge – Indo-Iranian, Anatolian, Slavic, Romance, Germanic, Celtic, Hellenic, Baltic and Albanian & Armenian.

The Indo-Iranian groups consist of Indic languages and Iranian languages. Indic languages include languages and dialects such as Hindi, Bengali, Marathi, Punjabi and Urdu but not languages such as Malayalam, Tamil, Telugu, Kannada or Tulu as these languages whilst geographically close, are thought to trace its lineage to Dravidian languages. The Iranian group consists of Persian, Pashto and Kurdish).

The Anatolian group of languages are thought to be extinct but may have indirectly influenced language development through trade and war. Anatolian languages include the Hittie, Lydian and other ancient languages.

The Slavic group can be separated into East, West and South Slavic. East Slavic includes Russian, Ukrainian and Belarusian; West Slavic includes Polish, Slovak and Czech; and South Slavic includes Bulgarian, Serbian, Croatian and Slovene languages. The Romance group includes the Spanish, Portuguese, French, Italian, Romanian and Catalan languages.

The Celtic group includes Irish, Scottish Gaelic, Welsch and Breton languages originating before 55BCE, with some researchers suggesting that there is evidence of Celtic languages that is over 3000 years old. The Hellenic group primarily includes ancient and modern Greek. Both the Celtic and Hellenic groups have been theorised to have had other languages as part of them, however, there is insufficient evidence in regards to what these would be.

The Baltic group includes Lithuanian and Latvian and are similar to the Slavic languages but are considered distinct enough by linguistics to be their own group. The Albanian and Armenian group are also considered distinct enough to be their own group of languages.

The Germanic group can be separated into three main groups – the East Germanic (now thought to be extinct and connected with the Goths from Scandinavia, the Vandals, the Langobards and the Burgundians), the West Germanic and the North Germanic (also known as Scandinavian). West Germanic includes English, German, Dutch and Afrikaans; and Northern Germanic/Scandinavian includes Swedish, Danish, Norwegian and Icelandic.

Indo-European languages differ in their syntax and morphology from Germanic ones, even though they all share a common ancestor. Latin and Greek have endings on nouns and verbs similar to Sanskrit, and some people will know these (e.g. the accusative -m) or recognise some of them in Modern German and Old English. Thus, the inflectional endings of Old English are due to its Indo European and synthetic origins.

As with most major languages the influence was spread initially by people of influence such as explorers, traders and militaries and later spread directly and indirectly through technology such as media and science. Modern English is messy but once a person understands what and how the various events influenced the language, the messiness begins to make some sense (Crystal, D., 2018).

Key War Influences

There were many conflicts that either indirectly or directly influenced the development of the English language. However the key war influences include the departure of the Roman Empire from Britain, The Germanic invasions of Britain, the Viking invasions of Britain, The Norman Conquest of Britain, the Hundred Years War, the English Civil War, the Napoleonic Wars, the World Wars (WWI and WWII), and various colonial (including trade missions) and post-colonial conflicts that accelerated the spread and diversification of the English language globally.

It has been argued that the wars that involved foreign forces invading Britain shaped the English language throughout the Early and Middle English periods. It has also been argued that the trade and colonising invasions influenced the development of the Modern English language through the bidirectional sharing of language. In this sense, conflict not only acted as a catalyst for linguistic change within Britain through conquest and cultural assimilation but also served as a vehicle for English expansion abroad, where contact with other languages, peoples, and power structures reinforced its role as a global lingua franca. Following the expansion of the American empire, the English language was solidified in its various forms as the global lingua franca (Mufwene, S. S., 2015).

Key Religious Influences

Key religious influences include the "arrival" of Christian missionaries, the translation of the Bible into Old and Middle English, the works of religious scholars such as Ælfric, Tyndale and Wycliffe, the Protestant Reformation, the publication of the King James Bible, and the rise of religious printing and pamphleteering in Early Modern Britain.

In the context of its impact on the English language development, The Protestant Reformation was potentially the largest religious influence. The Protestant Reformation refers to the breaking away from the Roman Catholic faith and the separation from the institutional authority of the Roman Catholic church. There were many factors that led to The Reformation with the main cited reasons including – King Henry the Eighth's desire to divorce from his marriage with Catherine of Aragon and the subsequent refusal by Pope Clement the Seventh, widespread dissatisfaction with the Catholic Chruch's corruption and abuses, Martin Luther emphasising personal faith and God's grace and the argument that people should be able to read the Bible for themselves in their native language, the rise of nationalism and the Printing Press.

The English Protestant Reformation, and the break with Rome, led to the need for a new version of the Bible that better reflected the social and vernacular needs of the time. This led to the need for a new version of the Bible that better reflected the social and vernacular needs of the time, which eventually led to the creation of the King James' Bible, largely based on Tyndale's work. Its widespread circulation and literary style helped standardise spelling, vocabulary, and syntax, embedding biblical idioms and rhythms into English prose and leaving a lasting imprint on English expression (Leith, D., & Graddol, D., 2006).

Media Technological Influences

Technological advances in industry, science, construction and other areas also allowed for the invention of various forms of media. The impact on language from the various media related technologies is enormous and ongoing. Media technological inventions included the Printing Press, Radio, Television, Internet, Social Media and more.

The most famous example of media technology impacting language development is the Printing Press. Due to the ability to produce large amounts of text more quickly, the Printing Press forever changed how many languages, including English would be recorded and communicated. Prior to the printing press, the monarch and church were able to dictate who was allowed to become literate. However, the printing press allowed for the spread of cookbooks, almanacs, sheets of music, how-to books, and after a lot of reformation, various versions of the Bible were printed in English. This also increased literacy rates during 1500-1700CE, with one estimate suggesting that 50% of the British population were literate (Berensmeyer, I., 2020).

The Printing Press was great for the mass production of written ideas. However, as happens with most world changing inventions, the Printing Press would be used for spreading disinformation and harming many people. It was used to spread fear and misinformation and used to control populations, with the most famous example including the witch hunts.

Daemonology manuals were printed on mass using the Printing Press reportedly describing witches, how to identify them and how to best prosecute them. The majority of these manuals were written by church officials, theologians, and university-trained scholars who were either part of the church hierarchy or closely aligned with religious institutions. The most popular ones included Malleus Maleficarum ("The Hammer of Witches") in 1487 by Heinrich Kramer on behalf of the Catholic church, De la démonomanie des sorciers ("On the Demon-Mania of Witches") in 1580 by Jean Bodin to honour the Catholic church, Daemonologie in 1597 by King James VI of Scotland (James 1 of England) to defend the persecution of witches to skeptics, and the Disquisitionum Magicarum Libri Sex ("Six Books of Investigations on Magic") in 1599 by Martin Del Rio who was a Jesuit priest. There were some influential people such as

Johann Weyer and Reginald Scot who used the Printing Press to challenge the witch hunts (Doten-Snitker, K., Pfaff, S., & Hsiao, Y., 2024).

The cultural and social ideologies during this period meant that women were targeted much more than men (approximately 85% of witches killed were women and 15% were men in Britain). Whilst, there was rarely legitimate reasons for this, the major reasons (looking through today's lens) include the following – women were seen as weaker, more lustful and more spiritually vulnerable meaning if a male were to be attracted to a person or complete a spiritually inappropriate behaviour, the only socially acceptable explanation was because the woman was a witch; women were more socially isolated and were easier targets; and women were much more likely to be midwives or herbalists which made them easier targets if bad things happened such as poisoning or miscarriage or if good things happened such as large groups of people recovering from illness (Sharpe, J., 2019).

The witch persecution did not directly change the English language through syntax or phonology; however, it did influence some of its development. It introduced and normalised supernatural, legal, and theological vocabulary, it influenced the themes and diction of Early Modern English literature, it helped shape the emotive and gendered language of sin, evil, and deviance and it left a legacy in idioms, metaphors, and political discourse. Print media remained the most influential form of media until the invention and widespread adoption of the radio (Clark, S., 1999)

During the early 20th Century, radio had become a dominant media and communication medium. In 1932, the BBC World Service British Broadcasting Corporation) assisted in spreading the English language around the world. The BBC promoted a standard form of spoken English and English culture. Many people who were learning English as a second language and people in colonised countries (who needed to or wanted to learn English), used the radio to help learn the standardised English language. The radio further encouraged a standard English through encouraging a standard way of sounding phonetically. The English language broadcast also led to entertainment such as music media incidentally spreading the English language and influence (Berensmeyer, I., 2020).

The Lumière Brothers' Motion Picture Camera (1895) ushered in the age of cinema, and with it, a powerful new vehicle for the English language was born. While silent films initially used intertitles that were easily translated, the arrival of "talkies" in the late 1920s gave spoken English a starring role on the global stage.

During the mid-20th Century, the English language became further assisted by the invention of the television (TV). The TV allowed many homes to observe British TV dramas, American TV dramas and sitcoms and eventually large budget movies from Hollywood studios in America. In many countries, some of the TV series became part of official and unofficial curriculum in language education. It also led to influence from video and jingle advertising, and added power to entertainment celebrities, all of which further increased the influence of British and American English (Berensmeyer, I., 2020).

During the late 20th Century, the invention of the internet led to a massive uptake of the English language through various influences (discussed again later). As the internet began to establish itself as a necessity in the modern world, it led to new ways of communication such as electronic mail eventually named E-mails. Emails accelerated informal writing styles, focusing on speed over standardisation accuracy and efficiency over detail. It allowed people to communicate with strangers all over the world almost instantly and allowed the sharing of information and ideas globally. Eventually the email technology and adoption led to other communication changes in the English language (Berensmeyer, I., 2020).

As the technology and use of the internet grew, a type of programming connection arose known as Social Media. Social media allowed many people to connect globally from the safety of their own homes (unlike emails, people were able to share information with the world by uploading this information for anyone to view), this in turn allowed a vast transfer of information that was more targeted but felt like social connection. This helped to spread American English much more quickly with the English language being the default language in most countries (Crystal, D., 2018). Many platforms arose each with a slight variance of their own, with some examples including Facebook (later rebranded as Meta), Instagram, Bebo, Hi Five, TikTok, Reddit, LinkedIn, Snapchat,

Myspace, and many other platforms, many of which came and went quickly.

The invention of Social Media being predominantly English speaking, led to the English language becoming the language used to help those of different language backgrounds communicate globally. It also led to an increased ability for advertising to become individually targeted (micro advertising), further connecting people to the English language. The use of visual language tools known as Memes increased the spread of the English language further. Finally, the invention of Hashtags in social media platforms further increased this spread and influence towards where it is today (Crystal, D., 2018).

Memes and Emojis

English is the first language to use visual language and Emojis and modern Memes are not the first use of shortened language.

Many ancient cultures used visual script languages such as the Indus Valley Civilisation, Minoan Civilisation, Hittie Empire, Olmec Civilisation, Mayan Civilisation and Egyptian Civilisation. The most famous to English speakers if often the ancient Egyptian Hieroglyphs. The Hieroglyphs are believed to have represented words, sounds and ideas. However, unlike the Emojis and Memes, the Hieroglyphs are thought to have been a complete writing system requiring trained scribes to understand and communicate, whereas Emojis and Memes form a part of modern communication within a larger picture. Fast forward to the 19th and 20th centuries and a shortened message invented for the telegraph, utilised reduced message lengths with only key words being sent, i.e. "Arrive Tuesday *STOP* Meet Station" *STOP*. Both systems demonstrated our ability to adapt and communicate to the current technological and social constraints and contexts

(Bennett, Ľ. L., Harišová, K., Formánková, A., & Joukl, Z., 2025).

Emojis are small digital pictographs that evolved during the 1980s and 1990s from digital text such as the colon and the close bracket :). They were often used to add depth, context or emotion in the new digital use of the English language, but they remained very basic. However, as technology improved and changed, so did the use of Emojis. The internet use of the words Meme began as units of cultural expression, often containing images with texts that were designed to be adapted, remixed and shared.

The use of emojis and memes enables people to blend visual symbols with written language, conveying tone, mood, and subtext while compensating for the absence of body language in digital communication. Their use led to changes in punctuation where the Emoji or Meme could be used as emphasis or to replace words or sentences within a conversation (or sometimes the entire conversation itself could be formed with Emojis and/or Memes. This led to non-English speaking people to interact with its use which, in turn, created a form of cross-linguistic communication that transcended traditional language barriers, allowing meaning to be shared without requiring full fluency in English. This phenomenon reflects earlier periods in history, when pictographic or symbolic systems such as early trade symbols, heraldic devices, or medieval merchant marks, allowed people from different linguistic backgrounds to exchange information, conduct business, and convey meaning without a shared spoken language (Crystal, D., 2018).

Other Technology Influences

The invention of the Telegraph in the 1830s to 1840s transformed long-distance communication by transmitting messages almost instantly through Morse code. Morse code is a telecommunications method that encoded text characters as sequences of short and long signals, known as dots and dashes separated by pauses. These represented letters, numbers and punctuation. Whilst Morse code is no longer in general use, it is still used today by select groups of people including but not limited to, radio operators, intelligence operators and even aviation.

The English language quickly became the dominant language of international telegraphy due to Britain's imperial reach and America's growing influence. This contributed to the spread of English technical jargon (such as "stop" for a period) and standardised brief, efficient writing styles that shaped modern business and news communication (Sylvia IV, J. J., 2024).

The updated invention of the Uniform Penny Post in 1840 built upon earlier successes such as the London Penny Post of 1680. It introduced in Britain, a national system that led to a surge in written correspondence, reinforcing literacy in English and standardised written forms of the language. As the British Empire expanded, postal systems modelled on the Penny Post spread, carrying English-language administration, commerce, and personal communication across colonies and trading partners Hanlon, W. W., Heblich, S., Monte, F., & Schmitz, M. B., 2022).

The invention of the Telephone in 1876 by Alexander Graham Bell enabled real-time voice communication across distances. The telephone accelerated the global spread of spoken English, as much of the early telephone infrastructure and corporate dominance came from English-speaking countries. Telephone switchboards and call protocols reinforced English business language, while telecommunication networks helped standardise certain phrases and etiquette in English that spread worldwide (Milne, G. J., 2007).

The Phonograph invention in 1877 by Thomas Edison allowed sound to be recorded and replayed, revolutionising the spread of language and culture. English-language songs, speeches, and educational recordings circulated widely, providing learners with models of pronunciation and accent. The phonograph also laid the foundation for the global music industry, where English lyrics and performance styles gained international prestige, strengthening English's role in popular culture (Camlot, J., 2019).

Food production technology advances in agriculture indirectly assisted the spread of major languages such as English. As agricultural technology such as harvesters, tractors and irrigation systems improved, it allowed for more people to move towards cities. This then allowed a sharing of ideas which quickly increased as population density increased. This also allowed for the indirect influence of food technologies through commerce. As the amount of food produced increased (thanks in part to scientists such as Norman Borlaug), the need to find larger and larger markets increased leading to international and later global trade, which indirectly influenced the spread of the English language, as well as the addition of industry specific language (Jargon) (Perkin, H., 2003).

Travel technologies such as ships, flight and motor vehicles led to a quicker spread of language. Ship technology such as the steamships in the 19th century CE, enabled quicker and more reliable travel across large ocean distances. This then allowed people to visit more places spreading language in a multi-directional pattern with major powers such as the English, setting up ports, needing shipping documents, inventing maritime laws and naval commands around the known world, and eventually globally (Pascali, L., 2017).

Flight technology such as the Boeing 707 in the 1950s, drastically reduced the time required to travel between vast distances. This meant people and products could now travel vast distances in increasingly shorter times, spreading language as they travelled. This also indirectly led to English speaking centres such as London and New York, which also then led to increases in international travel to and from these English-speaking centres (Djouhaina, C., 2022).

Other travel technologies such as the railroad, rail travel and eventually mass automobile production further increased access to travel, whilst reducing the time, and in some cases reducing the barriers to travel. Whilst English speaking countries like England and USA were still dominant at the time of the introduction of these technologies, it allowed versions of the English language to quickly spread globally (Balliet, G., 2013).

Key Spoken Art, Written Art and Author influences

Authors have had a lasting impact on the English language. There are several famous examples and some of these will be included here as examples. Words that are used only once, often invented by an author or playwright, are known as 'Nonce' words. They are often created by the writer with the intention of one-time use. However, overtime the initial 'Nonce' word can become accepted by others and become known as Neologism. A 'Neologism' is a word or phrase that is newly coined that hasn't officially entered common usage. Once words move into our common vocabulary, they become known as words (Crystal, D., 2014).

There are many examples of Nonce words that are now used and form part of our general vernacular. The word 'Nerds' was first introduced by Theodor Seuss Geisel known more commonly as 'Dr. Seuss'. Shakespeare has been credited with introducing over 1700 words with at least three hundred of these used as Nonce words (such as Tortive meaning twisted or winding) and at least 1000 words becoming common use in the English language such as Lonely, Bedazzled,

Dwindle, Eventful, Obscene, Manager and Laughable (Crystal, B., & Crystal, D., 2004).

In 1392 poet and author of 'The Canterbury Tales', Geoffrey Chaucer invented words such as twitter to try and explain very specific experiences that he felt that the current language of his time could not sufficiently explain (Berensmeyer, I., 2020). In 1667 author John Milton invented the word 'Pandemonium', used as the name for the capital of hell, also known as "the place where all the daemons lived". Overtime, the word has stayed but the meaning has shifted from the name of a capital city of hell, to meaning "a state of chaos", or "all hell has broken loose" (Wodak, R., & Forchtner, B. (Eds.)., 2018).

In 1819 author Sir Walter Scott invented the word 'Freelancers' meaning soldiers or mercenaries who did not fight for loyalty, rather for their own personal gain. The word remained, but the meaning shifted to mean "people who work job to job for different people or clients". In 1871 author Lewis Carrol invented the word 'Galumph' meaning a "triumphant gallop". In 1840 scientist Reverand William Whewell invented the word 'Scientist' meaning a "practitioner of the scientific method" (Garner, B. A., 2011).

In 1920 author Karel Capek invented the word robot to explain humanoid robots constructed to perform manual tasks. He reportedly borrowed the term from another word 'Robota' meaning forced labour in the Czech Republic. In 1937 JRR Tolkien invented the word 'Tween' to mean the period between a hobbit's life between childhood and adulthood (approximately 20 to 33 years old). The word is still used today but the age use has change to mean pre-adolescence (Horáková, J., & Kelemen, J., 2008).

In 1964 physicist Murray Gell-Mann repurposed the word 'Quarks' to name the hypothetical subatomic particles he proposed, which was originally used in 1939 by author James Joyce as part of a parody of a common cheer: Three quarks for Muster Mark instead of a more traditional toast three cheers for Muster Mark. In 1976 biologist Richard Dawkins invented the word 'Meme' meaning any shareable idea, style or behaviour, again, the word is still in use but its meaning has changed to "visual jokes that you share or communicate", often done online, which is still a type of cultural sharing (Blackmore, S., 1999).

As well as inventing words, authors have changed how we use words by combining or adding letters to change its usage, as well as adding prefixes and suffixes. The most famous author is again, Shakespeare, who has been credited with creating words via the combination of existing words such as 'bed' and 'room' becoming bedroom, and he has been credited with changing words usage from nouns to verbs such as noun 'gossip' into the verb 'gossiping'.

Conlang Influences

One slightly less obvious influence on the English language is known as Conlang (Constructed Language) both fictional and real-life attempts at an alternative language. While the history of English is rooted in conquest, migration, and cultural blending, its legacy lives on not only in global business and education, but also in the imagination. Nowhere is this more visible than in the rise of constructed languages, especially in fantasy and science fiction, with at least five hundred constructed languages to date.

Conlang are designed on purpose instead of the natural evolution of languages. Whilst it is theoretically possible for anyone to create their own Conlang, author Mark Rosenfelder believes a person or group needs to consider the phonetics, morphology, orthography, syntax and semantics for the language to be usable. Following this, it is believed that the conlang should be influenced by various existing languages so that it can borrow sounds and ideas from various cultures. Next the person or group needs to decide if it will be a language that utilises agglutination (a language that forms words by stringing together morphemes, where each morpheme typically represents a single grammatical function and retains its original form, also known as combining two distinct words to build complex words), SOV (Subject-Object-Verb), SVO (Subject-Verb-Object), or even Ergative-Absolutive-Alignment (a type of grammatical system to mark the roles of subjects and objects in a sentence) (Rosenfelder, M., 2009).

The most famous creator of conlangs is J.R.R. Tolkien. A philologist and Oxford professor, Tolkien didn't just write fantasy stories he invented languages first and then built a world around them. Among the most developed are Quenya and Sindarin, Elvish tongues featured in The Lord of the Rings and The Silmarillion. These languages have their own grammars, sound systems, and internal histories that are designed to reflect the cultures of the peoples who speak them. Tolkien's linguistic work showed that a fictional world could feel more authentic and immersive when its languages evolve organically, just like real ones (Salo, D., 2004).

His passion for ancient languages, particularly Old English and Welsh, deeply shaped the structure of his conlangs. Tolkien reportedly once said, "The invention of languages is the foundation. The 'stories' were made rather to provide a world for the languages than the reverse". Tolkien's influence has echoed through generations of storytellers and game designers. His legacy either directly or indirectly, inspired the creation of fictional languages in franchises such as: Star Trek (Klingon), Star Wars (Huttese, Shyriiwook, and others), Avatar (Na'vi), Game of Thrones (Dothraki and High Valyrian), Warhammer (Eltharin, Khazalid, and Chaos tongues) and World of Warcraft (Troll, Orcish, and Darnassian dialects). All of these conlangs have one thing in common, they were invented in the context of art (Rogers, S. D., 2015).

Fictional conlangs were influenced by English, but they have also influenced English. They have done this through creating words that slowly became accepted as English language including words such as 'Grimdark' and phrases such as "they are a real Jedi at coding". They have also influenced naming conventions for children, brands, usernames and fantasy world-building, increased interest in learning languages and influenced gaming and other digital and print art and design (Peterson, D. J., 2015).

Other conlangs have been invented with the intention to improve communication across cultures by having a universally accepted language. John Wilkins attempted to create a language that he believed was more logical and would therefore be more accepted, this later became known as 'Wilkins's Analytical Language'. However, his subjectivity regarding his classifications and lack of understanding of the fluent history of language might have led to its failure. However, his failure led to other attempts, most notably Esperanto.

In 1887 a book was self-published by a person calling themselves Dr. Esperanto meaning "one who hopes" and was a guidebook for international auxiliary language. Esperanto (L. L. Zamenhof) believed that this had the potential to be used as a backup language when interacting with people from different languages. Esperanto borrowed from existing Indo-European languages especially Romance, Germanic, and Slavic roots, allowing speakers of those languages to recognise patterns and vocabulary easily, to allow for the transition to be easier to learn and share. It currently has hundreds of thousands of speakers, with a small percentage who speak Esperanto as a first language. However, Esperanto never became the dominant global language its creator had envisioned. Despite its logical structure, ease of learning, and idealistic goals, its adoption remained limited. This outcome perhaps highlights a fundamental truth that language is not merely a tool to be engineered, but a deeply social and organic phenomenon (Tonkin, H., 2015).

Languages evolve over centuries through cultural exchange, historical events, and the collective choices of communities, not simply through design. The limited spread of Esperanto may suggest that language acquisition and preference are influenced more by natural sociopolitical dynamics and cultural identity than by utility or simplicity alone. This is exemplified by English currently being the dominant back up language for most of the world, following the cultural and historical influences of England and the United States of America as well as the technological influence such as the internet.

A famous Irish writer George Bernard Shaw highlighted the inconsistencies of English spelling saying the English have no respect for their language as demonstrated by how they taught the language to their children. One example he used was the spelling of the word fish as 'Ghoti'. He argued that using the English language rules the gh could be used as in the word enough, the o could be used instead of 'i' as in the word women, and the ti could be used instead of sh as in the word nation. His goal was for a new writing system for English, (not a Conlang directly) and he believed his idea would be revolutionary and helpful. He believed in his idea so much that he left money in his will, to devise a new writing system for English (Crystal, D., 2003).

In 1960 Kingsley Read developed the Shavian Alphabet. It consisted of 48 characters, each representing a distinct English sound (24 consonants, 20 vowels and 4 special characters. The hope that it would eliminate redundant letters, be purely phonetic and be more efficient. Despite how logical and helpful the Shavian Alphabet was there were several barriers to it becoming accepted. The first barrier was investment. There was no public or financial call for change and there was no major practical need for the shift (Wells, J. C., 1982).

Next the Shavian Alphabet required massive change at a time where American English had already established itself as the standard English socially and technologically and adopting the Shavian Alphabet was unneeded and costly and would require a total replacement not a supplement. The technology also meant that computing technologies could not handle non-Latin fonts, further reducing the efficacy of the Shavian Alphabet. Next there was no cultural attachment to the Shavian Alphabet, and many people felt that the alphabet looked too foreign and was not an upgrade. Many people reportedly did not see any benefit to learning another language that was not commonly known. Finally, it failed to take into account cultural, geographical and group differences in pronunciations of the English language, with there being no official phonetically standard way of speaking English (Wells, John C., 2000).

Other Key People and their Influences

There were many people and groups that influenced the development of the English language and whilst there are some such as Shakespeare who deservedly get a lot of attention, there were many others.

During King 'Alfred the Great's reign (849-899CE) he promoted literacy and translated many important Latin texts into Old English. He also helped to preserve English during the Viking invasions and help to lay the foundations for a written language tradition. Ælfric of Eynsham (955-1010CE) assisted by writing sermons and Latin-English glossaries. This helped to standardise Old English grammar and use in religious education (Blake, N., & Hogg, R. M. (Eds.)., 1992).

Walter of Bibbesworth (1235-1283) influenced the English language through his work "Le Tretiz", which was an instructional text to help teach the French language to English speaking children. His work helped to contribute to the bilingual language use, and helped future scholars and writers understand the transition from Old English to Middle English (Lerer, S., 2008).

During the Middle English period, John Wycliffe (1320-1382) produced the first complete English Bible (Wycliffe Bible), which assisted in advancing English literacy and religious reform and promoted the idea of English as a language of sacred texts. Julian of Norwich (1343) is the first known, or at least credited, woman to write a book in English. She wrote 'Revelations of Divine Love' which helped to normalise the use of English for religious and philosophical reflection. Richard Rolle (1300-1349) wrote spiritual works in English and Latin and help to establish the Northern English dialect as an acceptable medium for spiritual writing. Magery Kempe (1373) wrote 'The Book of Margery Kempe' which is credited as the first autobiography in English. It is one of the earliest extended Middle English texts that captured the speech and religious experiences of a woman (Blake, N., & Hogg, R. M. (Eds.)., 1992).

Thomas More wrote many works with his most famous known as 'Utopia', which blended classical Latin with English ideas and helped to define educated English writing during the Renaissance. William Tyndale (1494-1536) helped to translate large parts of the Bible from Hebrew and Greek into English, and his phrasing influenced many common biblical expressions still in use today. However, his work was considered by powerful people such as Sir Thomas More and Bishop Cuthbert Tunstall, to be heretical which led to his eventual execution (Daniell, D., 2001).

Richard Mulcaster (1531-1611) advocated for spelling reform and for formalised English education. He wrote 'The Elementarie' which promoted English as a respectable language for scholarship. Queen Elizabeth 1 (1533-1603) wrote many letters, speeches and translations (from Latin, French and Italian) into English which contributed to the prestige and expansion of the English language (Blake, N., & Hogg, R. M. (Eds.)., 1992).

Aphra Behn (1640-1689) is credited as being one of the first professional female writers in English, and wrote many playwrights, poems and novels, which helped to shape the English literature and introduce new narrative forms, colloquial dialogue and female voices into the English literary canon. Samuel Johnson (1709-1784) assisted in compiling 'A Dictionary of the English Language' which aimed to standardise spelling, definitions and use, and helped to shape dictionary making for future generations (Romaine, S. (Ed.)., 1999).

Ann Fisher (1719-1778) wrote 'A New Grammar' which was the first English grammar book written by a woman. She advocated for clarity and consistency in English use and argued for gender-neutral rules (such as "they" as a singular pronoun) (Rodríguez Gil, M. E., 2002). Robert Cawdrey wrote 'A Table Alphabeticall' which was written to help people understand difficult words that were borrowed from Latin and Greek. Johnathon Swift (1667-1745) advocated for language preservation and attempted to regulate the English language. Robert Lowth (1710-1787) wrote the works 'A Short Introduction to English Grammar', and argued against double negatives, split infinitives and ending sentences with prepositions. Hannah More (1745-1833) promoted widespread education and published moral essays and religious tracts in plain English. She advocated for accessible and simplified English in teaching and writing for children and non-elites (Hofrichter, F. F., & Yoshimoto, M. (Eds.)., 2021).

Emily Dickinson (1830-1886) was a poet who used unconventional grammar, punctuation and syntax that challenged and expanded the expressive possibilities of English. She helped to open the door to modernist experiments in form and function, showing that rules could be broken for emotional and artistic impact. Charlotte Yonge (1823-1901) was a novelist and linguist who published extensively and influenced Victorian English style. She compiled genealogical and historical glossaries, promoted an accessible (but elevated) form of English, and contributed to the Victorian era middle-class works. Henry Sweet (1845-1912) was a scientist who influenced modern linguistic study and inspired fictional characters such as Professor Higgins in 'Pygmalion'. James Murray edited the 'Oxford English Dictionary' and oversaw the systematic cataloguing of the English language's history and definitions (Wang, Y., 2023).

Beryle Atkins (1931-2022) was a lexicographer and linguist who pioneered corpus-based bilingual dictionary writing and was influential in the development of the 'The Collins-Robert English-French Dictionary'. She strongly influenced how modern dictionaries reflect real usage, not just norms and influenced how English is recorded and taught. Jean Aitchinson (1938) assisted with her work on language change and psycholinguistics, which helped to explain how and why English evolves.

David Crystal (1941) has written many works that helped to popularise the knowledge of English globally, including dialects and language change. Susie Dent (1964) is a lexicographer and etymologist who has championed lesser-known English words using TV and book media. She has written many works, and brings attention to regional dialects, historical vocabulary and assists the public to engage with the evolution of the English language (Johnson, K., 2024).

Industry Specific Jargon Influences

Many groups, either naturally over time or artificially through deliberate processes (or both), develop specific words and unique ways of using language to suit their context. While such linguistic changes are often assumed to remain localised, they can, in fact, extend beyond their original communities. Some of these words sometimes retained their original meanings, but often the words morphed into new meanings, eventually making their way into the primary language.

Sailing

There are many sailing terms still in use in Modern English, first arising during the 18th and 19th century as the English empire grew and spread throughout the globe. Words still used in Modern English include headway, bearings, fathom, awash, ahead, underway, fathom, skyscraper, logbook and figurehead. As well as words common phrases entered and remained in Modern English. Common phrases such as "to try a different tack", "giving a wide berth", "cut and run", "close quarters", "reaching the bitter end", "learn the ropes" and "passing with flying colours" (Sanleandro, M. P., 2015).

Medical

Medical terminology began influencing Modern English especially during the 17th to 19th centuries, as medicine evolved into a formal science and public health institutions developed. Many medical terms are derived from Latin and Greek but have transitioned into common usage. Words still used in Modern English include diagnosis, symptom, virus, contagious, immune, antidote, trauma, and placebo. Common phrases include "an ounce of prevention is worth a pound of cure", "under the knife", "clean bill of health", "pulse check", and "on life support" (Curtis, T. A., 2024).

Legal

Legal jargon has heavily shaped Modern English, especially through courtroom language, contracts, and political institutions. Many terms originate from Latin or Old French and became entrenched during the Norman and British legal traditions. Words include verdict, appeal, testimony, subpoena, witness, liable, acquittal, and hearsay. Phrases such as "beyond a reasonable doubt", "law of the land", "due process", "on the record", "case closed", and "loophole" are now widely used beyond legal contexts (Schneiderová, A., 2018).

Scientific

With the Scientific Revolution (16th–18th centuries), science introduced precision into language. As discoveries spread, so did technical vocabulary. Words such as gravity, theory, experiment, hypothesis, energy, and data now appear in everyday speech. Phrases like "light years ahead", "inertia", and "quantum leap" originated in scientific discourse but are now part of colloquial English (Schreiber, L., 2005).

Political / Diplomatic

Political and diplomatic language has shaped English through parliamentary systems, international relations, and media discourse. Words such as treaty, embassy, diplomat, sanction, coalition and policy are widely understood today. Common phrases include "playing politics", "red tape", "power vacuum", "spin doctor", and "sitting on the fence" (Maci, S., Demata, M., McGlashan, M., & Seargeant, P. (Eds.)., 2024).

Military

Military language entered common usage especially during wartime periods (e.g., Napoleonic wars, World Wars). Words include strategy, tactics, camouflage, frontline, deployment, rank, formation, and drill. Phrases like "bite the bullet", "call to arms", "on the radar", and "friendly fire" have been adopted into everyday conversations. As well as words, specific alphabet codes were developed during war time and later used in peace time and civilian roles (Georgieva, V., 2015).

The International Civil Aviation Organization (ICAO) phonetic alphabet, also known as the NATO phonetic alphabet, represents a standardised code in which each letter of the English alphabet is assigned a unique word (e.g., Alpha for A, Bravo for B, Charlie for C). While developed for global aviation and communication clarity, its roots and influence are deeply tied to military jargon and the broader evolution of English as a tool of global coordination.

During the early 20th century, especially throughout the two World Wars, the need for clear and unambiguous communication became urgent. Radio technology had made communication faster but was prone to interference, static, and mishearing, especially under stress, noise, or poor signal quality. Military operations required precision, and misunderstandings could lead to fatal errors. English, having become the dominant language of international air navigation and Western military alliances, was the natural foundation upon which such a code could be built.

Prior to the ICAO system, various phonetic alphabets were developed by different national forces. For example, the British Royal Air Force used one system, while the U.S. military used another. This disunity proved problematic during allied operations in World War II. For instance, the British used "Ack" for A and "Pip" for P, while the Americans used "Able" and "Peter," leading to confusion when relaying coordinates, aircraft call signs, or code names. Miscommunication during joint air missions and naval operations occasionally resulted in delayed responses, misdirected support, and even friendly fire incidents.

As a result, in 1956, NATO officially adopted a standardised alphabet based on earlier systems but optimised for international understanding. The result was a modified English-based phonetic alphabet designed for global pronunciation and minimal confusion across accents (Radul, S., & Kharlamova, L., 2023).

Each word in the ICAO phonetic alphabet was carefully chosen to be easily understood in noisy conditions and across languages. For example, "Juliett" was spelled with two 't's to ensure correct French pronunciation, while words like "Zulu" reflected a broader geopolitical awareness and neutrality. Though English-based, the system was intentionally global in its phonetic design. The alphabet's structure, vocabulary, and deployment in military and aviation contexts helped reinforce English's role as the de facto language of international operations.

In the context of military jargon, the phonetic alphabet also illustrates how Jargon can be used in the transformation of civilian English into specialised codes tailored for functionality. Terms like "Foxtrot" or "Tango" have since entered civilian usage in law enforcement, emergency services, and pop culture, further embedding military-originated English into the wider lexicon. For example, "Oscar Mike" (on the move) or "Charlie Mike" (continue mission) are now recognised in popular media, extending military speech patterns into everyday parlance (Radul, S., & Kharlamova, L., 2023).

Computer Technologies

Since the mid-20th century, computing and digital technologies have radically influenced English. Originally jargon, terms like interface, crash, upload, firewall, virus, browser, and debug are now mainstream. Phrases such as "go offline", "streaming content", "cloud storage", "hardwired", and "reboot" are now widely used (Greiffenstern, S., 2010.

Commerce

The rise of global capitalism and corporate culture brought jargon into general language. Terms like profit, leverage, stakeholder, merger, startup, synergy, networking, and scalable are frequently used beyond business. Phrases such as "think outside the box", "hit the ground running", "bottom line" and "in the pipeline" are now commonplace (Nunberg, G., 2001).

Sports

Sports from English speaking countries such as USA and Britain, especially boxing, cricket, baseball, and football, have contributed heavily to metaphorical language. Words such as goal, match, referee, pitch, score, foul, draft, and coach are now used in wider settings. Common phrases include "step up to the plate", "throw in the towel", "level playing field", "hit below the belt", and "down to the wire" (Nunberg, G., 2001).

Entertainment

Entertainment has coined many expressions that entered everyday language. Words such as script, cast, audition, role, scene, director, and production are common outside their origins. Phrases like "break a leg", "steal the show", "behind the scenes", "fade to black", and "in the limelight" are now part of general English (Nunberg, G., 2001).

Fashion

Fashion has contributed descriptive and metaphorical language, especially with the rise of media and advertising in the 20th century. Words like trend, style, designer, runway, couture, accessory, wardrobe, and label are now widely used. Common phrases include "fashion statement", "dressed to kill", "in vogue", "off the rack", and "out of style" (Nunberg, G., 2001).

Finance

Financial jargon became familiar during industrialisation, globalisation, and economic crises. Words include inflation, recession, stock, asset, interest, capital, portfolio, and credit. Phrases like "the bottom line", "broke the bank", "in the red", "cash flow", and "economic bubble" are now part of public vocabulary (Nunberg, G., 2001).

Aviation

Aviation terms emerged in the 20th century and often convey control, movement, or risk. Words like take-off, landing, airborne, and navigation are common. Phrases such as "flying blind", "on autopilot" and "grounded", have metaphorical uses in daily speech (Nunberg, G., 2001).

Construction and Architecture

Building and design terms have become useful metaphors in various areas. Words include blueprint, foundation, structure, framework, and cornerstone. Common expressions include "lay the groundwork", "build from the ground up", "under construction" and "brick by brick" (Farrokhi, F., Ansarin, A. A., & Ashrafi, S., 2019).

Music

Music has influenced emotional and structural expressions in English with words like rhythm, harmony, pitch, tempo and tone, commonly used beyond their musical roots. Phrases such as "offbeat", "march to the beat of your own drum", "change your tune", "in tune with", and "face the music" are widely used phrases today (Nunberg, G., 2001).

Artificial Intelligence

The field of Artificial Intelligence (A.I.), (especially since the 21st century) has already contributed significantly to Modern English. As AI research, robotics, and machine learning advanced, many technical terms entered public discourse. Words such as algorithm, neural network, automation, bot, deep learning, machine learning, model, prompt, and data set are now widely recognised.

In recent years, phrases like "artificial intelligence", "train the model", "natural language processing", "self-learning system", "AI-generated", and "the singularity" have moved beyond technical fields into education, business, media, and daily conversations. Figurative phrases such as "thinking like a machine", and "black box decision-making" reflect growing societal awareness and debate over the influence of AI in human life.

AI has also influenced language development through more subtle tools such as predictive text. Predictive text helps people to find appropriate words through suggestions and auto filling sentences. This increases the speed of written communication but also reduced the uniqueness of an individual's communication. In countries where the predictive text is English, it often suggested from the American English language model further increasing speed at the cost of individual language expression.

Another recent AI influence on language development involves AI generated content, often pulling from large language models available on the internet and summarising these based on prompts provided by the individual. AI still utilises computer speak (also known as binary code) initially but then utilises its training algorithms such as large language models to provide outcomes, often directed by user prompts. Again, efficiency and speed are increased at the cost of unique language expression. The potential negative of this loss of unique individual expression includes the homogenisation of language, where regional dialects, cultural idioms, and personal writing styles are gradually replaced by more standardised, algorithm-driven phrasing. Over time, this could erode linguistic diversity and reduce the richness of creative expression in both personal and public communication (Smith, G., Fleisig, E., Bossi, M., Rustagi, I., & Yin, X., 2024).

Old English – 450-1150CE

Historical linguists have noted that the complexity of a language's inflectional system often correlates with its age, isolation, and the number of native speakers. Older or geographically isolated languages, particularly those with small, stable populations, tend to preserve intricate systems of grammatical endings, cases, and verb conjugations. In contrast, languages that expand through trade, colonisation, or global use typically simplify their morphology to accommodate a wider range of speakers (Hogg, R. M., 1992).

For example, Old English was spoken by a relatively small and culturally cohesive population and was highly inflected, with noun cases, gender, and verb endings inherited from its Indo-European and Germanic origins. As English spread through conquest, trade, and empire, it absorbed vocabulary but shed much of its inflection, relying instead on fixed word order and helper verbs.

This broader pattern is observable beyond Old English such as dialects of Finnish, Hungarian, and Icelandic that retain their extensive inflectional systems within small populations, whereas globally spoken languages such as English, Mandarin, and Modern Arabic dialects tend toward analytic simplicity. Thus, linguistic expansion often brings morphological reduction, mirroring the social and geographic broadening of a language's community (Hogg, R. M., 1992).

Pre-Old English

Before the Romans arrived in Britain, Celtic tribes were the primary inhabitants of the British Isles. Their languages now largely extinct in England but surviving in Welsh, Irish, and Scottish Gaelic shaped early place names and some vocabulary. The Celtic languages are thought to have influenced English in three phases Loan words into Germanic, adoptions into Old English and a subtle influence after the Old English period.

The first phase of loan words include examples such as carrus 'wagon', lancia 'lance', and names such as Rhine, Danube, and Cognac. During the second phase the borrowing of words from Celtic to Latin and Germanic language in Britain are mostly nouns converted into Proper nouns – afon is 'river' and dwr is 'water'; when adopted, however, they become proper nouns — the rivers named Avon and the place names Dover and Dorchester. Similarly, Cardiff, Belfast, Kent, Thames, and London all derive from Celtic. These borrowings show occasional awareness of the syntax of Celtic. For instance, the name for Dover is originally Dofras in Old English since the original Celtic Dubris had also been plural. Landscape terms are borrowed frequently as well: cairn 'heap of stones', glen 'valley', loch 'lake', torr 'rock' or 'peak', dolmen 'rock', bar 'top', bre 'hill', llyn 'lake', and cumb 'deep valley' (Hejná, M., & Walkden, G., 2021).

In 55 BCE, the Romans under Julius Caesar began their conquest of Britain, bringing with them Latin. Though the Roman presence did not fully Romanise the British population, Latin words entered the language particularly terms related to administration, military, religion, and architecture. Examples include optimus (best), bonus (good), culpa (fault), pro (for), and bene (well). Around 200 Latin words were adopted during this time, although many were filtered through later languages before reaching English.

Like most languages of its time Old English was primarily an oral language relying on memory and communal knowledge transmission of what the shared language meant. It wasn't until the late 7th century that English moved from an oral heavy language towards a manuscript heavy language.

Germanic Influence

Old English was a Germanic (technically West Germanic) language spoken by Anglo Saxons, who were themselves unofficially made up of three groups known as the Angles, Saxons and the Jutes. After the Roman Empire withdrew its legions from Britain (410 CE), the island was left vulnerable to invasion. These Germanic tribes crossed the North Sea and began settling in eastern and southern Britain. Around 450CE the Germanic tribes arrived from regions that are now Denmark, northern Germany, and the Netherlands. When the Germanic tribes arrived, many of the native Celtic populations were pushed west into modern day Wales, North into modern day Scotland, Southwest into modern day Cornwall and some fled to Brittany (in modern day France) (Chomsky, N., 1965).

Old Norse, Latin and French

In 591CE Christian missionaries arrived and brought their Christian belief system to England during the seventh century CE, and they slowly replaced the original Runic alphabet (known as Futhorc) with the Latin Alphabet over approximately 150 years. However, this change did not happen naturally which, meant that a natural evolution of language did not occur. This led to several difficulties adapting the Germanic tongue to fit the Latin alphabet. One example is the extra work load some letters were given such as the letter 'C' making the 'K' sound and the 'Ch' sound. Some runic letters were kept such as Wynn (drawn to resemble a modern-day upper case 'P' and made the 'W' sound) and Thorn (drawn to resemble a modern-day lower case 'p' and made the 'Th' sound) (Blake, N., & Hogg, R. M. (Eds.)., 1992).

Following Rome's invasion, later withdrawal, and the arrival of Christian missionaries, the influence of Latin on the development of the English language becomes clear and is explored throughout this book. The most well-known influence on the English language is its loan words and the level of importance it held within Britain and the world for many centuries. The majority of the Latin loan words were commercial, military, religious, and cultural related terms.

The Latin influence on the English language is also visible today with the prefixes of 'Pro' (forward/in favour of) and 'Sub' (under or below) being initially borrowed by the Celtic languages and eventually being introduced again by the Christian missionaries. Words such as Promote, Progress, Proceed, Submarine, Subway, School and Subconscious.

In approximately 780-1040CE, Vikings invaded Britain, bringing with them cultural influences such as Norse mythology, shipbuilding technology, and a distinct Old Norse language. It is estimated they added around 2,000 words to the English vernacular, many of which remain in use today including Anger, Give, Freckle, Muggy, Sky, Egg, Law, and Window. Four of the current days of the week were names after Anglo-Saxon gods – Tuesday (Tiw in Old English named after Tyr from Norse mythology), Wednesday (Woden in Old English named after Odin from Norse mythology), Thursday (Thunor in Old English named after Thor in Norse mythology) and Friday (Frige in Old English named after Freya/Frigg in Norse mythology).

This invasion further concreted the need and use of written language with works such as Beowulf helping to spread the usage of the English language. The blending of Old Norse with Old English not only enriched vocabulary but also influenced grammar and syntax, accelerating the shift toward a more simplified inflectional system that would characterise Middle English (Blake, N., & Hogg, R. M. (Eds.)., 1992).

In 1066, William the Conqueror, Duke of Normandy, invaded England, won the Battle of Hastings, and installed French-speaking nobles to rule the country. French nobles began influencing the language starting with government, business, law, education and food names and spellings; however, the Latin languages were still used in church and the common population still spoke a version of English. The Norman invasion meant that many French words were brought to England with them but also led to the Norman and French scribes changing the spelling of many English words to what they wanted, to allow the words to look more familiar to French readers.

One of the first changes made was the removal of the remaining Runic letters, replacing the letter Thorn with 'Th' and replaced Wynn with two 'U's' which over time became known as the modern letter 'W'. They added letters to fit their spelling of sounds changing the spelling of words such as Hus and Hund to House and Hound, adding the 'G' to Night and Might. Norman-French scribes changed the spelling of 'kw' sounds from cw to qu. Following the rise of Parisian French influence in place of the Anglo-Norman French, words that were borrowed from the French languages often only had the 'k' sound in place of the kw sound like in words such as etiquette, physique, and unique (Hejná, M., & Walkden, G., 2021).

The Normans also changed the letter 'u' to 'o' in some words when it was followed by the letter 'v', 'n', or 'm', reportedly because in cursive writing it looked too similar to those letters, like in words such as come, some, love and son. However, this idea wasn't universally accepted such as the word drum. The Norman invasion led to an estimated 10 000 words being added to the vernacular still used today including Judge, Jury, Parliament, Slander, Evidence, Larceny, Access, Justice, Marriage, and Noble (Hejná, M., & Walkden, G., 2021).

For over 300 years, England was effectively bilingual with French spoken by the upper class, and English by the common people. Many French-Latin hybrids became common and bilingual words also emerged.

Old English Inflected Language and Grammar Rules

A lot of what we have learnt about Old English comes from the 2000 or more recipes, charms, riddles, descriptions of saints' lives, and epics such as Beowulf. Most remaining texts in Old English are religious, legal, medical, or literary in nature (Godden, M., & Lapidge, M. (Eds.)., 2013).

Old English texts are divided along geographic lines into Northumbrian, Mercian, West-Saxon, and Kentish and they can also be categorised in terms of whether they were written in early or late Old English and whether they are poetry or prose. Most evidence of older Old English comes from northern poetic texts such as version I of Caedmon's Hymn. Most evidence of later Old English comes from southern prose texts such as Alfred's Orosius or the works of Ælfric (Blake, N., & Hogg, R. M. (Eds.)., 1992).

The original works were written on vellum, a very expensive thin leather. Books were therefore owned by a monastery, a church, or a wealthy person and were typically versions of the Bible, prayer books, schoolbooks, manuals of various kinds, and music.

Most Old English texts, especially manuscripts such as Beowulf, use a modified Roman alphabet. This alphabet was introduced by Irish missionaries, and the letter shapes are not identical to those of Modern English.

Old English featured a rich inflectional system, vastly different from Modern English in structure and vocabulary. Inflection refers to the way words change form to express grammatical features such as tense, number, gender, mood, and case. In Old English, much like in Latin or modern German, word endings were crucial to understanding how a word functioned in a sentence. Nouns, pronouns, adjectives, and even some determiners were all inflected for case (nominative, accusative, genitive, dative), number (singular or plural), and gender (masculine, feminine, neuter). Verbs were also heavily inflected to indicate person, number, tense, and mood (indicative, subjunctive, imperative). For example, the word for "stone" in Old English could appear as stān (nominative singular), stānes (genitive singular "of the stone"), stānum (dative plural "to/for the stones"), and so on (Hejná, M., & Walkden, G., 2021).

This system meant that word order in Old English was more flexible than in Modern English because these endings made sentence roles clearer. Over time, especially after the Norman Conquest in 1066, this inflectional complexity began to erode. Influences from Old Norse (brought by Viking settlers) and Norman French, combined with natural internal simplifications in the language, led to the decline of inflections and the rise of a more fixed word order and increased use of helper words (prepositions, auxiliary verbs) to express grammatical relationships. This shift marked a major turning point in the evolution from Old English to Middle English, laying the groundwork for the more analytic and less inflectional nature of Modern English.

Since the spelling of Old English is closer to the actual pronunciation than that of Modern English, it is possible that the scribe said (f); however, it might also have been its voiced counterpart (v) since that is expected between vowels. Linguists think that Old English, like other languages, has voicing as a phonetic process. Remnants of this phenomenon can be seen in the pronunciation of wife, half, knife, and leaf with an f in word-final position but a v in the plural — wives, halves, knives, and leaves, between two vowels.

A second sound change that occurred in Old English is palatalisation (Brozovsky, E., Hinrichs, L., Ahlers, W., Bergs, A., Bohmann, A., Meemann, K., & Schultz, P., 2016). Starting in early Old English, the velars (k), (sk), and (g) are fronted, in particular before a front vowel (the velar sounds are not fronted before back vowels, as in cool). The Germanic skirt became Old English shirt, skatter became shatter, kirk became church, and egg became eye. Skirt, eye and egg still exist in Modern English because other Germanic languages did not undergo palatalisation, meaning when the Scandinavians came into contact with English, the English borrowed the non-palatalised versions. Some of these words come to co-exist (skirt and shirt), while in other cases one of the two forms 'wins' (Hejná, M., & Walkden, G., 2021).

Two other unofficial Old English rules were breaking, and vowel fronting. Breaking occurs when the front vowels æ, e and i become diphthongs (are broken into two sounds), before certain consonants, where the changes in spelling are indicated. Examples include – ald and half becoming eald and healf, werc becoming weorc, and Picts becoming Peohtas. This rule applies when the vowel is followed by an l or r and another consonant or when the vowel is followed by a h. Breaking is supposed to have taken place in Old English around the 7th century, especially in the South (in West Saxon). The fronting rule, also called i-umlaut, describes what happens when a back or low vowel such as o or u or a precedes an i. In Germanic, before English separates, the form for singular mouse is mus and plural mice is musi. The fronting of u to y occurs in the plural, before the plural -i, resulting in *mysi. The i-ending (having caused the fronting) subsequently disappears and the cause of the fronting becomes hidden (Hejná, M., & Walkden, G., 2021).

In Old English poetry, alliteration was a key feature. It means that important words in a line begin with the same sound. A typical line of Old English verse is split into two parts, often called half-lines. For example, in the line metudaes maecti end his modgidanc, the (m) sound begins three main words. This creates a strong link between them. Another line, uerc uuldurfadur sue he wundra gehuaes, shows a similar match in starting sounds, this time with (w).

Alliteration helped to shape the rhythm and memory of Old English verse. Unlike modern rhyme, which often links word endings, Old English poetry used matching starting sounds to hold the structure together.

Old English is a synthetic language (Inflection heavy), using a lot of word endings or inflections to indicate grammatical functions. The following are some common examples. The -as ending is a plural on some masculine nouns (nominative and accusative) and becomes the Modern English plural -s. The -e ending is a dative singular, -um the dative plural. Present tense verbs have a second person singular -st ending, and a third person -th ending and the infinitive ends in -an. Individual texts vary a great deal in orthography. For instance, hiene, hine, hyne are masculine singular accusatives, and hie, hi, and heo are third person plural nominative and accusative pronouns. There is a rare dual number (used for two people). Since the instrumental case is almost extinct in Old English, that form is left out.

Old English third person pronouns show masculine, feminine, and neuter gender. Unlike Modern English, Old English also marks grammatical gender on demonstratives, adjectives, and nouns. The grammatical gender of the noun determines the gender of the demonstrative and the adjective. Thus, the masculine forms of the demonstrative and adjective are used before masculine nouns such as cyning 'king'; the feminine forms are used before feminine nouns such as lufu 'love'; and the neuter forms are used before neuter nouns such as godspel 'gospel'. The grammatical gender did not always correspond to the natural gender of a noun such as wif 'woman' and cild 'child' are neuter .

Reflexive pronouns, such as myself and himself, do not occur in Old English, except in later texts. Instead, the regular pronoun is used for both subject and object, such as hē hine lufode ("he loved him", where hine refers back to hē). In Old English, the adjective self is typically used as an emphatic intensifier, as in ic self ("I myself"). Self-marked reflexives first occur with the third person in later Old English. There is much variation across texts and dialects.

Old English demonstratives are often translated by using the Modern English article "the", even though they are quite different. Unlike Modern English articles, demonstratives are not generally required and carry more information. The indefinite article a(n) is not used, but sometimes the numeral ān ('one') or the adjective sum ('some') are. Again, be aware that the þ is used as the first consonant of the demonstrative, as well as the s in the nominative masculine and feminine plural, such as þā stānas ("the stones") (Hejná, M., & Walkden, G., 2021).

In Old English, demonstratives are often used where Modern English uses relatives. Relative pronouns connect one sentence to another by linking a noun to a clause, as in sē mann, þe ic geseah ("the man whom I saw"). Old English words such as folc and frōfor, were later replaced by French loans, and the g in geong ("young") and geardum ("yards/dwellings"), which later becomes a palatalised (j) sound, reflect broader phonological shifts (Hejná, M., & Walkden, G., 2021).

Nouns have endings for number, case, and gender. Endings such as those on the noun stān ('stone') are the most common noun endings, since most nouns belong to that class. This class is called the a-stem, and stān is a masculine noun of that class. There are other genders and noun classes: word is neuter (and belongs to the same a-noun class), lufu ('love') is feminine (o-noun class), and sunu ('son') is masculine (u-noun class). In Indo-European, the noun actually ends in -a, -o, or -u (or some other ending), but this is no longer visible in Old English (Hejná, M., & Walkden, G., 2021).

The plural ending of stanas later becomes the general English plural -(e)s, and the Old English genitive -es becomes the possessive in the dog's bone. Word has the same endings as stan, except in the nominative and accusative plural. We can still see the result of this lack of an ending in the plural of deer and sheep — deer and sheep. Note that even though lufu 'love' is feminine and sunu 'son' is masculine (and of a different class), they are very similar in endings. The ending of the adjective is very intricate in Old English. As in other Germanic languages, such as German, Dutch, and Swedish, its form depends on whether a demonstrative is present.

This is different in the other Indo-European languages. If no demonstrative precedes the adjective in Germanic, the adjective gets a more distinctive (strong) ending to 'make up' for this lack; if the adjective is preceded by a demonstrative, it gets a less varied (weak) ending. The strong and weak endings are also referred to as indefinite and definite in some Old English grammars.

Adjectives are used in comparative and superlative constructions. In Old English, the pattern for hard and narrow is heard, heardra, heardost and nearu, nearora, nearwost respectively. These are inflected forms, typical of a synthetic language. The analytic forms with more and most are rare in Old English.

In Old English, adverbs are formed by several different endings: -e and -lice (which later becomes -ly) such as rihte ("rightly") and freondlice ("in a friendly manner").

The endings on verbs depend on the tense (past and present), the person and number (of the subject), and the mood (imperative and subjunctive). They are divided into strong and weak, but these terms are used differently than when describing adjectives. Strong verbs change their stem vowels in the past tense and the past participle. The stem vowels in the present are long, but short in most of the past forms.

In Old English, pronouns often occur near the beginning of the sentence, whereas verbs often occur at the end, especially in subordinate or embedded sentences. Subject pronouns are somewhat more optional in Old than in Modern English.

Past action is indicated through affixes, such as the -on suffix for the past plural, and also through the (aspectual) prefix ge-, as in past participles like "geworden" (become) or "gefundon" (they found).

Connecting of sentences occurred in two main ways in Old English: by parataxis (placing clauses side by side without conjunctions) and by subordinating conjunctions such as þæt (that), þonne (when), and gif (if).

Adverbs in Old English, as in present-day English, can be used to express the mood of the speaker and are then considered discourse markers. Examples include soþlice ("truly"), witodlice ("certainly"), and la ("indeed" or used for emphasis).

The negative adverb often immediately precedes the verb and is sometimes weakened to a prefix. In addition, multiple negatives can occur such as ne geseah he naenne mann ("he did not see no man").

The most surprising aspect of Old English is how Germanic the vocabulary is compared to Modern

English. From Old English to now, it is estimated that 80% of the original vocabulary has been lost.

Many Old English words also use prefixes such as ge- and ofer-, suffixes such as -ung, and compounds with -lic. Many of these still occur in Modern English but some have a broader or different meaning in Old English: wiþceosan means 'reject' (choose against), and wiþcweþan means 'deny' (speak against).

Old English and early Middle English also formed questions differently to Modern English. Old English formed questions by inverting the verb and subject, and negation was expressed with ne before the verb such as "Ne seah ic þæt" ("I did not see that"). During the late Middle English period it changed to what we know today, a do-support negation and question such as – "Do you like it?, I do not know" (Hejná, M., & Walkden, G., 2021).

Middle English – 1150-1500CE

Simplified English

Old English does not abruptly change on 1150CE, it instead develops into Middle English over a period of time being influenced technology, cultures, disease and the resulting social changes. The reason 1150 is chosen here is that written texts have been found that are definitely much more 'modern' in having lost many of the endings and in starting to make use of grammatical words. The year 1500CE is chosen as the end of the Middle English period because by then most grammatical changes have taken place and the Great Vowel Shift is under way. An external reason for this date is that book production changes dramatically.

During the Middle English period, many of the language inflections began to be replaced with extra words and spelling patterns that clarified grammatical relationships such as word order, auxiliary verbs, and prepositions marking a shift from a synthetic to a more analytic language structure.

During the Middle English, various influences on the language arose leading to an increase in literature which exhibited the language's developing richness and versatility (Chandra, P., & Verma, P., 2024).

Black Death

One theory about what led to the Great Vowel Shift was the Black Death and its impact on labour shortages. Some studies have suggested that approximately forty percent of the clergy and approximately thirty percent of the general population died from the plague. The survivors increasingly felt the burden of surviving which led to discontent leading to the Peasants' Revolt in 1381. This led to an increase importance to the labouring class and in the importance of labouring jobs (Baugh, A., C., & Cable, T., 2002).

This labour shortage and increased social and economic importance placed on labouring jobs, led to people from various areas in England moving to London seeking opportunity. This then led to dialect mixing which naturally caused a vowel shift. Examples provided by this theory include people "overshooting" their pronunciation of vowels as well as prosodic changes in the Germanic languages being influenced.

Norman French Influence Decline

For over 300 years after the Norman Conquest in 1066, England was effectively bilingual. French remained the language of the ruling elite, government, and law, while English persisted among the common people. Many French and Latin words entered English during this time, and spelling conventions were altered by French scribes. However, English continued to evolve, absorbing and adapting. Over time, tensions between the English and French intensified, both politically and culturally, setting the stage for a linguistic resurgence of English.

During the Hundred Years' War between England and France, English nationalism surged. As a result, the English language began to reclaim its prominence in court and official settings. By the late 1300s, English re-established itself as the language of government and law, albeit heavily altered by centuries of French and Latin influence (Decker, D., & Sumanasekara, S., 2025).

Regional Dialect Diversity

A large regional dialect difference began to emerge during the Middle English period. As centralised control over language weakened and local communities became more isolated, regional dialects developed with increasing variation in vocabulary, pronunciation, and spelling. The lack of a national education system and the limited use of English in formal writing meant that there was no single "standard" English during this time. Instead, dialects such as Northern, West Midlands, East Midlands, Southern, and Kentish became highly distinct.

For example, the word for "she" was heo in Southern dialects, sho in Northern dialects, and she in Midlands dialects, which that eventually became standard. Similarly, the past tense of "make" varied from made to maked depending on the region (Richards, O., 2018). Even everyday words such as church could appear as kirk (Northern), chirche (Southern), or churche (Midlands). These differences made communication between speakers from different regions more difficult and contributed to the richness and complexity of Middle English texts (Hejná, M., & Walkden, G., 2021).

Sound changes are very regional as well. For instance, palatalisation does not occur in the North either and thus, we have non-palatalised forms like Frankis, kirk, and egg where southern texts might have French, church, and eye 'egg'. Many of the northern forms still survive in the North in the modern period.

Writers like Geoffrey Chaucer, who wrote in the London-based East Midlands dialect, helped that variety gain prestige over time. Eventually, due to the political and economic importance of London, the East Midlands dialect (influenced by both Northern and Southern forms) became the foundation for Early Modern Standard English.

Whilst there wasn't a large push for standardisation just yet, during this time there were several examples of regions suggesting their version as the more acceptable version of English. The most well known example is the East Midlands dialect being increasingly used for administrative and literary purposes in the late 14th century, partly because of its central location and influence of London, and some scribes promoting it as more 'universal' than Northern or Southern varieties.

Middle English Influences, Changes and Rules

It is thought that only after 1300 does English reemerge as a language used for literature, the court, and the church. Several historical dates are relevant to this reemergence: 1244, when it becomes illegal to hold land in both France and England; 1258, when Henry III uses both English and French for an official proclamation and English gradually gains influence; 1349, when English is first used at Oxford University; and 1362, when Edward III opens Parliament in English. Prior to approximately 1300, using English had to be defended, however, after 1300 there is a social shift, and many texts are written in English.

Middle English texts available are varied: songs, travel accounts, recipes, medicinal handbooks, saints' lives, sermons, philosophical and scientific works, romances, and fiction. There are several plays, such as the Wakefield and York Cycles; government documents prepared at the Chancery; anonymous lyrics; works of the Gawain poet, John Wycliff, Margery of Kempe, and Julian of Norwich; William Langland's Piers Plowman; Geoffrey Chaucer's extensive writings; and letters written by members of prominent families. We have the Paston Letters (1420s–1503) and the letters of the Cely (1472–1488) and Stonor (1290–1483) families, which show a dialectally consistent transition between Middle and Early Modern English (Hejná, M., & Walkden, G., 2021).

Some Middle English works provide an idea of daily life in the towns and castles, churches and monasteries. During Middle English, the æ and ð spellings are replaced relatively early by a and th/þ, respectively. In late Middle English, þ is replaced by the th used in French sources; before it is replaced, however, it starts to look like y, hence the writing of the ye in ye olde shoppe. Each Middle English text is somewhat unique. For instance, v and w are introduced, but their use is different from text to text: vppen 'up' and wiues 'wives' in Layamon. Respelling is a result of the Renaissance realisation that Latin has th in those words even though Middle English and French do not. Notice the difference between French auteur and English author (Burchfield, R. (Ed.)., 1994).

The main theme in Middle English is consonant deletion, as in the case of (g), (h), (w), and (l), and vowel shifting, especially in non-northern texts. The Great Vowel Shift hadn't yet occurred, so in words such as April, soote, bathed, and seeke, the vowel is pronounced as if it were French or Spanish. There are many sound changes between Old and Middle English (Hejná, M., & Walkden, G., 2021).

This g sound first becomes a w or y and blends with the vowels before it to form a double vowel, or diphthong, and the word foweles and plow show this shift (Burchfield, R. (Ed.)., 1994).

The loss of (h) begins in consonant clusters such as hlaf 'loaf', hraðor 'rather', hnutu 'nut', and hnacod 'naked' and gradually the version without h becomes the norm. This may be due to French influence. The glide (w) is frequently deleted between a consonant such as (s) or (t) and a (back) vowel. In Modern English spelling but not pronunciation w turns up again in some words. In Middle English, the situation is not settled.

In Middle English, the short vowels change their height and are not just short variants of the long vowels. Where short and long vowels have the same position, the long vowel is differentiated by a colon. Some (a:) sounds change to (o) (or (ow)), as noted above, and the round front vowel, spelled y, as in hydan 'to hide', ultimately becomes an unrounded (i)

The Middle English pronouns undergo many changes. First, the Old English third person plural pronouns with an initial h- are gradually replaced by ones with an initial th-. The change starts in the Northern parts of Britain with the nominative such as they.

Secondly, a special feminine singular sho/she is introduced. This change too starts in the North.

A third change is the second person pronouns are used differently in Middle English than in Old and Modern English. In Old English, thou and thee are singular and ye and you plural. In Middle English, the singular becomes the familiar form, similar to French tu, and the plural becomes the polite form, similar to French vous.

Other differences include – all duals are lost early on, and the accusative forms mec, þec, usic, eowic, hie, and hine disappear early. Only the accusative hine survives into Early Middle English. An example of this is He sloh hine ("He slew him").

Third person special reflexive pronouns begin occurring in Late Old English, and first person and second person special reflexive pronouns begin appearing in Middle English. Middle English also retains the regular pronouns such as I, thou, he, we, ye, they.

Old English adjective self is reanalysed by learners in Middle English as a noun with a possessive my or thy. The third person has an accusative pronoun him before self because it changed when self was still an adjective modifying a pronoun. The first and second person reflexives were formed when self was a noun, so my, thy, our, and your are possessives. Common examples include myself, thyself, himself, ourselves, yourselves.

During Middle English we see a major reduction of forms and endings regarding demonstratives, relatives, adjectives, and nouns. The case endings of demonstratives, adjectives, and nouns simplify in this period and the number of different forms decreases.

In Late Middle English, definite and indefinite articles, the and one/a, become frequent, as do two demonstratives indicating number — this/these and that/those. In Modern English, the indefinite a is used before words starting with a consonant and an before words starting with a vowel (a table, but an object).

Nouns still have a genitive singular ending -es but very little else. In the plural, the Old English nominative and accusative -as simplify to -es for all cases in Middle English. In Early Middle English, there are some dative nominal endings in -e, especially after prepositions. Common examples include to husbande, and on erthe.

Adjectives, like demonstratives and nouns, have lost most endings by Late Middle English. This starts in the North and the East Midlands. The last remnant of an ending is the -e in this goode man, or the supposedly archaic ye olde shoppe.

Adjectives can occur in the comparative (synthetic nicer or analytic more interesting) and superlative (synthetic nicest or analytic most interesting) and the shift towards an analytic language is expected to result in more "more" and "most" forms. In Middle English, these analytic forms are indeed on the increase. These changes during Middle English demonstrate the change in the English language from synthetic language to analytic language (Burchfield, R. (Ed.)., 1994).

The word order in Middle English is still relatively free, compared to Modern English. However, with the grammaticalisation of prepositions, demonstratives, and some verbs (which become indicators of case, definiteness, and tense), a stricter order is established. For instance, articles can only occur before nouns and auxiliaries before verbs. Sentences that ignore this rule during Middle English often had French influences (as the French language often placed the adjective after the noun).

Yes/no questions are occasionally introduced by "whether", (also reduced to wher in some sentences), a remnant of Old English. Most of the time, the word order is like Modern English except that the main verb can be in sentence-initial position such as Went he to the market?, rather than just the auxiliary (Burchfield, R. (Ed.)., 1994).

There is also a transition during Middle English to nominative subjects such as he, she, and I. Pleonastic subjects become more common as well, as seen from Chaucer's example "Ther is at the west syde of Itaille / Doun at the root of Vesulus the colde...". This demonstrates the language is in a more analytic stage. There is grammaticalising from a locative adverb to a placeholder for the subject.

In Early Middle English, the pleonastic subject is still optional, such as in "Is" in the hous a man. In Old and Middle English, auxiliaries are less frequent than in Modern English.

In Early Middle English, the connection between sentences is similar to that of Old English: sentences are less frequently embedded in each other than in Modern English. Common examples of this in Middle English include and he wente, and for he was wroth.

In Middle English, reinforcement by a post-verbal adverb such as nawiht ('no creature') is frequent, as shown in Middle English. Subsequently, the post-verbal negative becomes the regular negative not or nat, especially in late Middle English. An example sentence would look like I ne seye nat this ("I do not say this").

Multiple negatives are lost in Late Middle English, but the negative "not" starts to contract with an auxiliary, e.g. cannot, as early as 1380. The negative weakens and a second negative is introduced again in many varieties of English. This is known as Jespersen's Cycle after the Danish linguist who first discussed it.

Definite articles are frequent and reduced to an invariant form þe. The endings on the nouns are restricted to plural -eš, -ez, or -es, but there may be a dative -e on erþe. Examples include þe kinges wordes, þe churches, on þe erþe. These reflect common Middle English plural and dative forms such as kinges (plural genitive or possessive of "king"), wordes (plural of "word") and churches (plural with -es ending)

Compounding words is frequent in both Old English and Early Modern English but appear to be less frequent during Middle English, possibly because of the wealth of loan words during the Middle English period.

Word meaning changes accelerated during Middle English, potentially because of the amount of loan words. Beginning and commencement are synonyms in Middle English. When commencement first comes into the language in 1250, it means 'time of beginning' and this meaning remains a minor one. By 1387, commencement is attested as meaning 'taking the degree of Master or Doctor'. Commencement

Day is first attested in 1606. When French and Latin words enter the language, they are often in competition with 'native' words. This can lead to the borrowed words narrow meaning narrowing, as in the case of commencement, adolescence, and adoration. Most words have shifted their meanings and you can track that using the OED (Burchfield, R. (Ed.)., 1994).

Regional Dialect Diversity

Dialectal differences are more obvious for Middle English since there are more texts available from the different areas. The differences are also obvious because a Middle English standard had not arisen yet so that pronunciation differences are often clear from the spelling of words (McIntosh, A., Samuels, M. L., Benskin, M., Laing, M., & Williamson, K., 1986).

Many dialect differences are obvious because the sound changes in Old and Middle English did not have the same impact in all areas. For instance, palatalisation of the velar stops (k) and (g) is a southern Britain phenomenon as is the voicing of initial fricatives in words such as vather and the change of long "a" to "o". The fronting of the fricative (w) to (s), on the other hand, is typical of the North. Thus, more sound change seems to occur in non-northern areas.

Changes in the morphology are the opposite, where the loss of endings starts in North Britain as does the replacement of third person pronouns and the marking on the non-finite forms, such as participles and infinitives. Sound and spelling differences included the palatalisation of velars, Fronting of "y" sounds, Long a becoming o, Short on-an ending differences voicing of starting consonants and the spelling of hw and qu. Palatalisation of velars in Northern Britain has no known changes ("frankis" keeps the hard k and g sounds). In the Midlands some words stayed similar to the North where others changed to a softer sound like j. In Southern Britain changes more strongly to soft j sounds (a k sound might become j). Fronting of "y" sounds – in the North the "y" sound became s, as in "sal"; in the Midlands it was mixed between s and y sounds; and in the South it stayed a y sound ("shal" has a soft beginning). Changes with the long a becoming o – in Northern Britain the Middle English long a remained ("ham"), in the Midlands it mostly changed to o, and in the South it fully changed to o ("home"). For short on-an endings the North used "on" endings like "mon", the Midlands used both "on" and "an", and the South used "an", as in "man". The voicing of starting consonants (f and s) saw changes – the North and Midlands began with unvoiced sounds like f and s, and the South changed to voiced sounds like v and z. Lastly for spelling of "hw" and "qu", the north used "qu-", and the Midlands and South used "hw-" (Gelderen, E., 2006).

There were regional differences in morphology and syntax as well. For third person plural pronouns (they/them etc.) the North used "they/them", the Midlands used "they/hem" and the South used "hi/hem". The Feminine third person singular (she) in the North was "she", in the Midlands was "she" or "heo" and in the South was "heo". Verbal present tense endings in the North added -es or -s, the Midlands had mixed forms and the South were closer to Old English with more complex endings. For present participle (doing, going) the North words ends in -ande, the Midlands ends in -ende, and the South ends in -ing or -inde.

For past participle (spoken, gone) the North had no prefix, and the Midlands and South used prefixes like y- or i-. For infinitive markers (to speak, to walk) the North used "to", and sometimes "at", and the Midlands and South used "to". Finally the use of the preposition "till" the North used it and it appeared early during the Middle English period, whereas the Midlands and South used it but it appeared much later (McIntosh, A., Samuels, M. L., Benskin, M., Laing, M., & Williamson, K., 1986).

The North kept many older, simpler forms and had fewer changes to sound. The South developed more new spellings and endings, while the Midlands showed a mix of the two. These differences show how spoken and written English varied a lot by region during the Middle English period. However, not all changes predict geographical origin, but geography has been used to help track the development of the language (Rissanen, M., & Lass, R., 1999).

Early Modern 1500-1700CE & Modern English 1700CE to Present

In Old and Middle English, scribes used a modified Roman alphabet to transcribe their own speech or to copy from other manuscripts. This meant only a select few could afford and be trusted with the transcriptions. There is also often a lot of variation within the writings of one scribe as well as between different scribes from the same area: sealm, selm, salm, spalme, sphalme and many others are listed in the Oxford English Dictionary (OED) for 'psalm'.

The Early Modern period is difficult to date exactly. It depends on whether we take political events such as the Restoration (of the British monarchy) in 1660, or other external dates to be important. The year 1700 has been chosen by linguist historians because the Great Vowel Shift is nearly complete, spelling is mostly standardised, and English speakers start to spread the language around the world. After 1500CE the first English dictionaries and word lists begin appearing but do not yet reflect how the spoken language is used. Some scholars argue for another period of English language development known as the Late Modern English period. I have chosen not to do this as there is too much disagreement between when this period begins with 1800 – present and 1900 – present being the two most common.

Whilst there is no written or recorded evidence that I could find that openly transgender individuals have historically shaped the grammar or structure of English like early male and female authors and writers, transgender and nonbinary voices have significantly influenced modern English usage. Through advocacy, literature, and online activism, they have reignited the evolution of gender-inclusive language by repopularising singular they, coining new identity-related vocabulary, and prompting major institutions to revise how English reflects human diversity. In this way, contemporary trans authors and communities have influenced the ever-changing use of language in the Modern English language, with the decentering of gendered norms in pronoun use and identity expression being some of their largest modern contributions.

Early Modern English

In Early Modern English, capital letters are used more frequently than in Middle English, where they only occur at the beginning of the line, if at all. The punctuation during Early Modern English is still stylistic rather than grammatical. This use of punctuation is characteristic of a language that is not yet completely analytic.

A cultural shift during the Early Modern period also occurred and influenced language development. The shift to the Renaissance influenced language development with a major social-cultural theme being 'celebrate the day' instead of the previous medieval idea of 'remember that you will die'. This more optimistic worldview encouraged greater creativity, expressiveness, and individuality in writing, which led to the expansion of vocabulary, increased use of metaphor and classical references, and the elevation of English as a prestigious literary language. The other major cultural shifts during the Renaissance were the freedom of ideas and the logical analysis influenced by the increased importance of science and mathematics (Romaine, S. (Ed.)., 1999).

The transition from Middle English to Early Modern English was marked by a series of significant phonological, grammatical, and sociolinguistic changes. Many of these developments helped shape Modern English as we know it today. Among the most notable were the changes in consonant pronunciation, vowel sounds, grammatical forms, word stress, and pronoun usage.

One of the prominent phonological shifts during this period involved the loss of the consonant r in certain positions. Already disappearing in Middle English, r began to be dropped before consonants, especially in southern English dialects. For instance, words like arse and bærs evolved into ass and bass. This tendency led to variation in spelling and uncertainty about when to include the letter r, as shown in 15th-century documents like the Cely Letters, where parcel appears as passel. By the late 18th century, this loss of post-vocalic r resulted in a divide between rhotic and non-rhotic accents, which still defines many English dialects today.

Another important sound change involved the pronunciation of final -ing. In Early Modern English, it was often pronounced with n (as in runnin) instead of the velar nasal (ing) found in words like sing. This distinction had already existed in Old and Middle English, where (ing) appeared before velar stops, but not at the ends of words. Over time, the contrast between words like sin and sing became clearer in some varieties of English, introducing (ing) as a regular final sound.

The pronunciation of initial (h) also underwent substantial change. In earlier periods, (h) was dropped before certain consonants, such as in the transition from hlaf to loaf, or hnitu to nit. Later, h was lost before glides in many dialects, eliminating the distinction between words like which and witch. This shift became socially significant, with the absence of h being considered non-standard or lower-class after the 18th century. This social pressure contributed to the pronunciation of h in words like history, hospital, and hymnal, despite their lack of h in the French words they derive from.

Changes also occurred in how speakers chose between a and an, and my and mine. These choices depended on the sound that followed. If the next word began with a vowel or earlier h, the form ending in n was used (e.g., an eager air, mine own eyes). Otherwise, a or my was preferred. This system remained stable for articles until the present day and for possessives until about the 18th century. The purpose of the n ending was to ease pronunciation between words.

Word stress patterns also shifted significantly. Old and Middle English typically placed stress on the first syllable, following Germanic rules. However, the increasing use of multi-syllable Latin and French words introduced different stress patterns. Words like academy, acceptable, and corruptible began to place stress on later syllables. While some older stress patterns persisted until the 18th century, overall, the trend moved toward the more variable stress rules of Modern English.

Grammatically, Early Modern English saw a greater resemblance to Modern English as the Great Vowel Shift neared completion. It also featured a general loss of inflections and an increase in prepositions and auxiliary verbs, reflecting the language's move toward an analytic structure. Although this process was partially halted by prescriptive grammarians, without their intervention the third person singular -s ending and case distinctions in pronouns (e.g., I/me, she/her, who/whom) might have vanished entirely (Romaine, S. (Ed.)., 1999).

Pronoun usage during the Early Modern English period reveals sociolinguistic nuances. The distinction between thou/thee and ye/you was once a marker of social relationships and politeness. Unlike the strict tu-vous system in French, English usage was more flexible. For example, in Hamlet, Shakespeare uses thou to express Hamlet's disdain for Rosencrantz and Guildenstern, while you is used in more formal or neutral situations. This change reflects broader cultural shifts and social stratification in language use.

One linguistic innovation of the period was the development of the neuter genitive form its. Previously, English used his for the genitive of it, a usage occasionally found even in Early Modern English. The form its likely arose by analogy with possessive pronouns like hers and yours. Both its and it's coexisted into the 18th century, though only its survives in standard grammar today, while 'it's' is now exclusively a contraction for it is (Romaine, S. (Ed.)., 1999).

Reflexive pronouns, such as himself and myself, were still developing during this time. Earlier English used simpler forms like him selfe or simply him. The eventual adoption of reflexives marked a shift toward more complex pronoun constructions, paralleling the broader grammatical evolution of English.

Further evidence of morphological simplification includes the loss of the second person singular verb ending -st, which was tied to the decline of thou. Similarly, the third person singular ending -th (e.g., he hath) was replaced by -s (e.g., he has), a change that became widespread by the end of the Early Modern English period. Finally, subjunctive forms were increasingly replaced by modal auxiliaries and infinitive constructions, as seen in expressions like should go, might be, or to see.

Verbal agreement in Early Modern English is often 'wrong' by prescriptive standards. This lack of clarity on the part of the speaker and writer is in keeping with the move towards an analytic language and the disappearance of agreement (and case).
Comparatives and superlatives in Early Modern English can be doubled: most unkind est, more richer, and worser.

Adverbs do not consistently end in -ly yet, and the distinction between strong and weak verbs is different in Early Modern English. For example, in the sentence "And his great Loue ... hath holp him", holp is a strong verb, and in the sentence "They shaked their heads" shake is a weak verb. During Early Modern English, there were still many words that in different contexts could be verbs, nouns, adjectives, adverbs or prepositions, such as "love", "fast", "round", and "light".

Towards the end of the Early Modern English period, the language was almost transformed into the analytic language we know today. This transformation leads to an increasingly fixed word order and the introduction of grammatical words. An example of a grammatical word being formed is the directional to becoming a dative case marker. In Middle English, the number of prepositions and determiners increases as prepositions replace cases. Starting in the Early Modern English period, the grammatical words introduced are mainly auxiliaries. The trend towards more embedded sentences that started in Middle English also continues in Early Modern English.

Auxiliaries are introduced or expanded, but neither simple auxiliaries nor sequences of auxiliaries are as elaborate as in Modern English. The expression of tense, mood, and aspect is perhaps still the most important difference between Early Modern and Modern English. The end of the Middle English period is also when auxiliaries begin to be contracted, which is expected as they grammaticalise into true auxiliaries. This development is evident in the Cely Letters, the Paston Letters, and the late 17th-century writings of John Bunyan.

In the 17th century, syntactic punctuation is introduced, especially through the work of Ben Jonson. It is one of the changes modern editors make when editing Early Modern English texts for a present-day audience. When the language gets a strict(er) word order, it is natural for writers to punctuate according to grammatical function (Romaine, S. (Ed.)., 1999).

The Great Vowel Shift

The Great Vowel Shift (originally coined by Otto Jespersen) occurred approximately between 1350-1700 CE. During this time the pronunciation of many English vowels changed with no clear reasons existing today that explains this. What we do know however, is that this vowel shift, led to the pronunciation still used today in modern English. Examples include – the 'ou' sound changing to 'ow', the 'ah' sound changing to 'eh' and the 'ee' sound changing to 'ai'. Many words lost a syllable such as words like name and like moving from two to one syllable, with the second syllable instead being represented with a silent letter such as the 'e' in name and like, the 'b' in dumb, the 'gh' in night and light, and the 'k' in knife and knight (Wolfe, P. M., 1972).

"Name" in Middle English, sounded more like "nah-meh", whereas today, we say "name" with a long "ae" sound. "Sweet" in sounded more like "swayt", whereas now it sounds like "sweet" with a sharp "ee" sound. "Great" sounded more like "greht", whereas now it's "grate". "Time" sounded more like "teem", whereas today we say "time" with an "eye" sound. "Boot" sounded more like "boh-teh", whereas now it's just "boot" with a long "oo" sound. "Boat" sounded more like "bawt", now it's "boat", and finally "House" sounded more like "hoos", and now it's "house" with the "ow" sound.

The Great Vowel Shift didn't affect all vowel sounds and words right away, with some vowel sounds still not in their modern pronunciation until 1600CE. The following are examples of approximately how and when the main vowel changes occurred in Britain. For (i) (as in "ice") the changes followed the approximate timeline of 1400 said like "ee" in "see", 1500 changed to something like "ey", and 1600 closer to "ey" and 1700 and Modern English changed to "ai" in "ice". For ee (as in "meet") the changes followed the approximate timeline of 1400 said like "e" in "bed", 1500 changed to "i" in "machine", and 1600 to Modern English stayed the same as in "ee" in "see".

For ea (as in "meat/great") the changes followed the approximate timeline of 1400 & 1500 sounded like "e" in "bed", 1600 sounded like "ey", and 1700 and Modern English said either "ee" in "meat" or "ey" in "great". For a (as in "ace") the changes followed the approximate timeline of 1400 such as "a" in "father", 1500 changed toward "e" in "bed", 1600 like "e" in "bed", and 1700 and Modern English like "ey" in "face". For ou (as in "out") the changes followed the approximate timeline of 1400 like "oo" in "boot", 1500 changed to "ow", 1600 changed to "w" sound, and 1700 and Modern English: Like "ow" in "now". For oo (as in "boot") the changes followed the approximate timeline of 1400 like "o" in "go", 1500 changed to "oo" and remained the same for 1600 to Modern English. For oa (as in "boat") the changes followed the approximate timeline of 1400 & 1500 like "aw", 1600 like "o", and 1700 & Modern English like "ow" in "go".

While pronunciation changed dramatically, spelling did not keep pace. Some scholars at the time wanted to drop the silent letters to represent the updated pronunciation, however the Printing Press halted this (Wolfe, P. M., 1972).

Grimm's & Verner's Laws

As well as the Great Vowel Shift, there was also a great consonant shift, known as Grimm's Law. Named after Jacob Grimm (one half of the famous Brothers Grimm) this linguistic law outlines a systematic transformation that occurred between the Proto-Indo-European (PIE) language and its descendant, Proto-Germanic, the ancestral tongue of English, German, Dutch, and other Germanic languages (Ringe, D., 2017).

Grimm's Law was first systematically described by Rasmus Rask, a Danish linguist in 1818 who noted that certain consonants in Greek, Latin and Sanskrit corresponded to different consonants in Germanic language. However, it was Jacob Grimm who formalised the pattern in 1822 in his *Deutsche Grammatik*. Grimm observed that certain consonants in Germanic languages consistently corresponded to different consonants in non-Germanic Indo-European languages (Lerer, S., 2008).

At the time, this was a radical idea. Language change was often viewed as irregular and chaotic. Grimm's work helped establish the field of historical linguistics and demonstrated that sound change is systematic and predictable, laying the foundation for the comparative method still used in linguistics today (Ringe, D., 2017).

It describes a set of regular, systematic consonantal changes that occurred as the Proto-Germanic languages evolved from Proto-Indo-European (PIE), around 1000–500 BCE. These sound shifts affected stop consonants, and they are consistent across nearly all Germanic languages, including Old English. Grimm's Law identifies three major shifts – Voiceless stops to Voiceless fricatives (voiceless plosive sounds p, t, k becoming the fricatives f, th, h), Voiced stops to Voiceless stops (the PIE voiced plosive sounds b, d, g becoming p, t, k in Proto-Germanic), and Voiced aspirated stops to Voiced stops (unaspirated) (voiced aspirated stops bh, dh, gh became regular voiced stops b, d, g in Proto-Germanic).

Not long after Grimm's Law was introduced, scholars noticed that there were some exceptions. For instance, not every p became f, and not every t became th. This puzzle was explained by Karl Verner, who described a related pattern now called Verner's Law in the year 1875.

He showed that the way a word was stressed in PIE affected how the sounds changed. For example – PIE bhrater (with stress on the second part) became Germanic brother and PIE phater (also with stress on the second part) became Germanic father.

In both cases, the stress placement changed how the sounds developed. Verner's Law helped explain these details and worked alongside Grimm's Law to give a more complete picture of how Germanic languages evolved.

Grimm's Law is often one of the first concepts taught in historical linguistics courses because it demonstrates regularity in language change, demonstrates how phonology evolves systematically, and provides insight into etymology and language comparison.

For English speakers, it answers the question of why related words look and sound so different. Why is it three in English but tres in Spanish?

Grimm's Law systematically accounts for the transformation of Indo-European consonants into the patterns we see in modern Germanic languages, including English. The law explains why many English words diverge so dramatically from their Latin or Greek relatives, and it underscores the deep history embedded in the simplest of words father, foot, heart and brother.

By tracing these patterns, linguists can reconstruct ancient languages, map linguistic families, and understand how cultural contact and internal developments shape the sounds of human speech. For English speakers, Grimm's Law offers a glimpse into the profound and often invisible forces that have shaped their language across millennia (Ringe, D., 2017).

Jespersen's Cycle

While Grimm's and Verner's Laws explain the systematic changes in consonant sounds from Proto-Indo-European to Proto-Germanic, Jespersen's Cycle addresses a very different aspect of linguistic evolution: the development of negation in English (Wallage, P. W., 2017).

Danish linguist Otto Jespersen (1860–1943) observed that many languages follow a recognisable pattern in the way they express negation over time. This process, now known as Jespersen's Cycle, outlines a three-stage transformation that helps explain how the grammar of English — particularly negative sentence structure — shifted from Old English to Modern English.

Jespersen's Cycle identifies three stages – Simple Negation, Reinforced (Double Negation) and Replacement of the Original Negation. Simple Negation occurred when a single word is used to express negation such as in Old English, Reinforced (Double) Negation occurred when a second negative element is added for clarity or emphasis such as in Middle English, and Replacement of the Original Negation occurred when the original negative (ne) drops out, leaving the second element (not) to carry the meaning such as in Modern English.

Just as Grimm's Law revealed the systematic nature of sound change, Jespersen's Cycle revealed that grammatical change, particularly in negation, follows a regular, trackable path.

At the time, it was common to think of grammatical change as irregular or stylistic. Jespersen showed that even function words and sentence structure develop in predictable, cyclical ways, shaped by logic, emphasis, and communicative clarity (Wallage, P. W., 2017).

Pre-Printing Press Standardisation

Prior to the invention of the Printing Press, an unofficial standard of spelling in English began to emerge. Scribes working at the Chancery in London began writing in English (rather than Latin) in 1420 and, by the 1430s, a standard had evolved. The Chancery produced a huge number of documents, and this was connected to the rise of London as a major centre for trade and politics. Chancery English is characterised by relatively free spelling, but some rules evolved such as gh at the end of high even though the consonant is no longer pronounced, th endings for third person verbs, as in he doth 'he does' even though many varieties already have 'he does' and many other variations of the very rules they were trying to establish (Berensmeyer, I., 2020).

Migration patterns into London (often from the Midland north of London) led to the rise of a middle class which in turn generated scientific and religious texts, that still did not represent a majority of the population but began to cement an unofficial standard of English spelling and grammar.

The printing press also influenced the way capital and small letters were used and understood. The distinction between majuscule (capital) and minuscule (small) scripts already existed in manuscripts, but printers physically stored them in separate type cases. Capital letters were kept in the 'upper case' and smaller letters in the 'lower case,' giving rise to the terminology we still use today. Because lowercase letters were more common, they were placed in the easier-to-reach lower drawer. Over time, the printing press helped standardise not only the shapes of letters but also the rules of capitalisation, such as using capitals at the start of sentences and for proper names (McKitterick, D., 2003).

Printing Press Influences on Outdated Sounds and Hypercorrections

In 1440 Johannes Gutenberg invented the printing press in Germany. Within 100 years it had spread across most of Europe. This meant that the languages had to become standardised to enable the use of the printing press.

However, the people in charge of standardising the language had their own motives regarding the spelling and letter choices of the English language, even if these were not commonly accepted by the public at the time. Dutch type setters added letters to fit their own Flemish rules and conventions such as adding the letter 'h' to ghost, whilst other changes were accidental hypercorrections such as adding the silent 'b' from the word dumb to other words such as limb (from lim), crumb (from crum) and numb (from num). During this period the Renaissance had also become a major influencer regarding what was considered the correct way to spell words and what words counted as common or higher-class English (Crystal, D., 2018).

The addition of these higher-class words borrowed from French, Greek and Latin became known by the common folk as Inkhorn words referring to the inkpots and the people derogatively termed "know-it-alls", used to write words. The people in charge of writing during this time were heavily influenced by the Renaissance and added letters to words to pay tribute to their etymological roots based on rules they developed such as etymological Greek words having the 'h' added to words starting with 'C' such as Chaos (from Caos), and changing the first letter from 'f' to 'ph' such as Physics (from fysics); etymological Latin words had silent letters added purely as a reminder of the words' heritage such as Debt (from det), and Receipt (from receit).

Hypercorrection also occurred during the printing press changes. Silent letters were incorrectly assigned to words who they wrongly assumed the etymology of such as adding the 's' to Island (from Iland which had connections to the Old English word Igland) who they wrongly assumed was etymologically connected to the word Isle (which had connections to the Latin word Insula). The end of the Great Vowel shift led to the end of Middle English and the Beginning of Modern English. The printing press concreted over

1000 years of natural and unnatural language corrections into what is known as English today (Crystal, D., 2018).

Transition Away from Gendered Nouns

Old English, like many other Germanic languages, originally made extensive use of grammatical gender. Nouns were assigned one of three categories masculine, feminine, or neutral and this affected their noun, verb, determiners, and pronoun use. Importantly, grammatical gender in Old English did not always correspond to natural gender. For example, the word for "woman" (*wīf*) was grammatically neutral, while "maiden" (*mægden*) was also neutral, and "sun" (*sunne*) was feminine (Curzan, A., 2003).

As English evolved into Middle English (c. 1100–1500), the influence of Old Norse and especially Norman French began to erode the complex system of grammatical gender. The loss of inflectional endings, a defining feature of the shift from Old to Middle English, also contributed to this simplification. Without distinct endings to mark gender, case, and number, many of the grammatical distinctions began to fade.

By the Early Modern English period (c. 1500–1700), grammatical gender had mostly disappeared. English nouns were no longer gendered based on arbitrary classifications. Instead, natural gender began to dominate nouns referring to males used "he", those referring to females used "she", and inanimate objects or abstracts used "it." This shift marked a significant divergence from most other European languages that retained gendered nouns.

In English, the use of "they" as a singular pronoun, dates to at least the 14th century and was used by prominent authors such as Chaucer, Shakespeare, and Jane Austen to refer to an unspecified person when the gender was unknown or irrelevant. By the 18th and 19th centuries, grammarians insisted that 'he' should be used as the default singular pronoun, arguing that 'they' was grammatically incorrect when referring to singular antecedents.

This shift was largely pushed by male prescriptive grammarians influenced by Latin grammar rules, which lacked a gender-neutral singular pronoun. Whilst Latin grammar rules was the official reason, some linguist researchers strongly suggest that the patriarchal society reinforced by influential male scholars was the actual reason.

This is exemplified by the change that happened with Anne Fisher's grammar book. In 1746, Anne Fisher's grammar book allowed for they as singular and this was officially accepted as normal English grammar use. However, by the late 1700s and 1800s, prominent grammarians like Joseph Priestley and Lindley Murray insisted that he be used as the default.

This grammar rule paralleled the broader cultural shift that was happening at the time across the legal, political, and educational domains, which all increasingly used male-centred language to exclude or marginalise women. The idea that "the masculine embraces the feminine" became a formal grammatical principle.

Feminist linguistic activism in the 1970s to the 1990s challenged the assumption that masculine pronouns were neutral. Scholars such as Robin Lakoff and Deborah Cameron highlighted how language reflected and reinforced gender bias. This led to widespread promotion of gender-neutral alternatives (police officer instead of policeman, chair instead of chairman), and the revival of the singular they as a non-gendered pronoun.

From the 1990s onward, LGBTQ+ communities played a central role in pushing for pronouns that reflect a diversity of gender identities. There goals were to mainstream the use of they/them as personal pronouns for individuals, introduce neopronouns such as ze/hir, xe/xem, and others, and creating gender-neutral titles like Mx., (which appeared in print in the late 1970s and gained dictionary recognition in the 2010s). These movements reframed pronoun choice as a matter of identity and respect, linking language change to social justice and human rights (Curzan, A., 2003).

This resurgence of singular they in the late 20th and early 21st centuries was driven both by a return to its historical use and by new social needs. Today, "they" serves two functions – the generic singular (for indefinite or unknown individuals such as "If someone knocks, tell them to wait"), and for the specific singular (for individuals who identify outside the gender binary such as Alex said they would be here at six).

Its formal acceptance has accelerated with Merriam-Webster naming the singular "they" its Word of the Year in 2019, with their data finding a three hundred percent increase in online use of the singular "they". Style guides such as the APA, Chicago Manual of

Style, and Associated Press now endorsing it also helped to accelerate its acceptance (Saguy, A. C., & Williams, J. A., 2022).

Classism ('Inkhorn') Social and Capitalist Influences

Mass standardisation arose because of the Printing Press and its ability to quickly mass produce. Standardisation was not a neutral process and instead was heavily influenced by Classism also known as Inkhorn influences. The changes helped to establish a structure but was heavily influenced by the ruling elite rather than the most common usage of the language, with 'London English' becoming the Standard of English. Whilst some influential people were motivated to improve the English language and improve access the mass, the standardisation led to the use of language being used as a social tool of exclusion ("the haves" knew how to speak correctly, and the "other" or "common folk" knew not how to speak correctly). This social use of the correct form of spoken English has continued through to recent times with the easiest example being Academia where one idea is openly preached by lecturers but a "standard" use of spoken English is reinforced through various non written assessments and unspoken criterion (Smith, J. J., 2006).

The rise of the importance of the Nation State led to the Tudor (1485-1603) and the Stuart (1603-1714) dynasties overseeing the centralisation of English power which included the consolidation of English as the national language. This period saw the growth of bureaucratic record keeping, the standardisation of spelling and grammar in official documents, and the increasing association of the English language with national identity and political authority (Baugh, A., C., & Cable, T., 2002).

Between 1582 and 1610 the first full Catholic Bible was translated from the Latin Vulgate (which was itself translated in approximately 405CE and contained a mix of literal translation from Hebrew and Greek and Artistic licencing using clarity, rhythm and elegant prose) into English, by English exiles such as Gregory Martin and William Allen in France. Its style was full of apparent direct borrowings from the Latin vocabulary and phrasing. It added words such as holocaust (a burnt offering), evangelise, advent, acquisition and communion. This allowed many people to connect to a faith that may have benefited them. Unfortunately, many readers of this and subsequent versions did not understand its translation history and misused the phrasing to control, attack and influence various groups of people.

In 1611 the 'King James' Bible' was translated from Hebrew (Old Testament), Aramaic (Old Testament passages) and Greek (New Testament) to English by 47 scholars (who were reportedly experts in the three biblical languages) organised in six groups with 2 in Oxford, 2 in Cambridge and 2 in Westminster. It also consulted earlier version of English translations such as William Tyndale's work and the Latin Vulgate. This translation was not an accurate language translation and instead aimed for a balance of accuracy, and artistic licence to interpret the original message during the translation process. The King James' Bible translation was written using a poetic and rhythmic style that used memorable phrasing and metaphors which made it easier to read and share. The rhetorical structure also allowed the church and others in position of power, to portray a sense of authority, solemnity and morality.

Alongside the Printing Press, The King James' version assisted in standardising the English language at the time, promoted a common form of the English language and assisted in establishing English as the language of worship in most of Britain. The King James' version was more influential than previous bible translations and also allowed many people to connect to a faith that may have benefited them. Again, many readers of this and subsequent versions did not understand its translation history and misused the phrasing to control, attack and influence various groups of people.

In 1660 the Royal Society of science was formed. Initially Latin was still used as the primary language, however in 1665CE the Royal Society began publishing Philosophical Transactions, (the first scientific journal in the world), and by the 1790's English had replaced Latin as the dominant language of communication within the Royal Society.

Shakespeare influenced the English language through his extensive amount of written works (including plays, poems, and sonnets) where he has been credited with adding approximately 1700 words to the English language. Beyond vocabulary, his works shaped English grammar, expression, and idiomatic usage. His creative manipulation of syntax and metaphor contributed to the flexibility and richness of Modern English. During the 18th century,

Shakespeare's works indirectly led to the spread of the English language to non-English speaking countries, where his works were widely translated and studied, becoming essential reading in education systems around the world, thereby helping to spread both the prestige and usage of the English language internationally. His work also challenged the standardisation process by using multiple spellings for words and names.

In 1755 a lexicographer Dr. Johnson published a dictionary containing almost 43 thousand words in an attempt to solidify a "correct" form of spelling words. His dictionary included etymologies, example sentences, and quotations from literature, such as Shakespeare and Milton. This assisted print publications, education and public institutions to have consistent agreed upon spelling.

In 1857 the Oxford English Dictionary (OED) was started and in 1928 it was finally finished. The OED aimed to be descriptive, documenting every known word in English, with historical development, earliest use, and spelling variants; included over 400 000 words with quotations from literature, law, science and everyday usage, and their authority and influence at the time further reinforced a "correct" and standardised way of spelling used in publishing, education, everyday use and academia of the Commonwealth countries (Baugh, A., C., & Cable, T., 2002).

As England expanded their empire globally, a multi-directional language exchange took place. The Caribbean gave words such as Barbeque and Cannibal, India gave words such as Yoga, Shampoo and Bungalow, Africa gave words such as Zombie and Trek, China gave words such as Ketchup, and Australia gave words such as Nugget and Boomerang. British English became standardised despite the natural evolution of language that continued occurring, and it wasn't until the rise of the United States of America that the standardised spelling was challenged on a large scale. Migration heavily influenced the use of English in English speaking countries with many new words developing such as Chur (used to express thanks or approval) in New Zealand, Smoko (a short break) in Australia and Jaunt (A short Journey) in South Africa (Romaine, S. (Ed.)., 1999).

Animals and Food

As well as standardising words, spellings, grammar, etc., Social and Class often influenced English in more niche ways such as animal group names and food names. Different groups of animals have different names, and this is known as the 'Terms of Venery'. This has minimal purpose other than class and social status. It was originally used as a way for groups of people to identify the "real hunters" during the 1300-1500s, as a tool to cement ones own social status or highlight the lack of social status of another, examples include a "parliament of owls", a "murder of crows" and a "shrewdness of apes". In 1486 the first edition of the Book of Saint Albans published a list of collective nouns for various animals, hunting and heraldry, as well as included group names for non-hunting related groups such as a "sentence of judges" and "a melody of harpers" (Crystal, D., 2014).

Food name changes based on political opposition rarely last (such as "freedom fries" or "liberty cabbage"), however, the etymology of food names do have various cultural and social influences. To start, the word 'food' can trace its origins to the Proto-Indo-European word known as pa (pie – meaning to feed). The word 'corn' was at one point given to many different forms of grain. This then led to the word 'peppercorn' which was the name given to the small berries of the Piper Nigrum plant because of their resemblance of grain. Pepper became a very popular seasoning and finding more even became a major influence behind the funding Christopher Columbus received from the Spanish Monarchy. Columbus instead found chillis in Mexico and the Caribbean which were renamed chilli peppers because of the popularity of pepper in Europe, despite chilli and pepper being unrelated biologically.

Meat names have also been heavily influenced by cultures and social language. The name for pig, cows and sheep were used by the common or lower-class people when tending the animals, however, when wealthy French nobles ordered the meat to eat, they named them porc (pork), beof (beef) and moton (mutton). Wild animals such as deer became named venison which is connected to the French word 'venesoun' meaning the meat that was just hunted.

Some foods were named to increase the uptake of food such as Sweetbread which sounds like a delicious desert potentially covered in sugar, but is actually cooked animal glands, with some thinking the 'bread' part of the word might have originally referred to an old English word 'braed' meaning flesh or meat. Some fish that had gross sounding names were renamed for sales including Orange Roughy (for slimehead), Chilean Sea Bass (for toothfish), Pacific Snapper (for rockfish), Bombay Duck (for lizardfish) and Mahi Mahi (for dolphinfish).

With the adoption of capitalism, many foods were named or renamed to increase sales including fruits and other foods. The fruit commonly known as the 'Kiwi Fruit' originated in China and was originally known as Mihoutao and Qiyiguo. Once they were imported to New Zealand in the 20th century, they were originally called 'Chinese Gooseberries' as they tasted somewhat like Gooseberries. However, fifty years later when they were exported to northern America they didn't sell well and the name was blamed. Various name changes were tried including Melonettes (as they looked like small melons), however, eventually they were named after the well-known native New Zealand bird the Kiwi Bird. Social associations with a food product can also influence sales. The prune which is great for digestive health was originally popular with older people, and over time became negatively associated with old age. The sales of the product reduced, and the name was changed to 'Dried Plum' which increased sales very quickly. However, as the social influences moved towards health foods, the name was changed back to 'prune' as the modern society now saw the benefits of good digestive health for all ages and not just the elderly population. The prune is a great example of the interplay between the social influence and the capitalism need to make money.

Other foods were named as a cultural insult such as 'Welsch Rabbit' which is melted cheese on toast. Some linguists believe that the term 'Welsch Rabbit' was used as an insult towards Welsch people from the English, calling them so poor that their rabbit had no rabbit in it (Crystal, D., 2014).

Math Influence on English

During the late 17th century and early 18th century, intellectuals across Europe emphasised reason, order, and scientific thinking. Thinkers such as Isaac Newton, John Locke, and René Descartes influenced a cultural shift toward valuing precision and unambiguous expression, including in language.

Grammar was increasingly modelled on mathematical principles, especially logic. In formal logic, two negatives cancel each other out such as in "Not unhappy" = happy. Prior to the late 17th century, double negatives in English were okay and sometimes even encouraged as a form of emphasis.

However, the increasing social influence of mathematics and logic changed the English language and strongly influenced standardisation of the language specifically with a specific focus on standardising grammar rules. It was thought by many of the ruling elite, that if the English language became standardised, that it would be more logical and therefore lead to a society that became more rational. They believed that this would improve society (Wallage, P. W., 2017).

Beginnings of American English Influence

Noah Webster pioneered a more phonetic spelling of the English language which was later championed by the 'Grammatical Institute of the English Language' in 1783 and the book 'An American Dictionary of the English Language' in 1828, which led to the American English version of Modern English.

As the United States emerged as a global power, the influence of Noah Webster's 1828CE dictionary also expanded. His dictionary advocated for a system of simplified, phonetic spelling that aimed to make English more logical, consistent, and uniquely American. Over time, Webster's reforms became standard in the U.S., and as American political, economic, and cultural influence grew so did their global reach of American English spellings (Romaine, S. (Ed.)., 1999).

English and its Modern Variants

Kachru Three Circles Model

In 1985 linguist Braj Kachru developed a model that divided English into three circles (Inner, Outer and Expanding).

The Inner circle included current "native speaking" countries such as the United Kingdom, the USA, Australia, New Zealand and Canada (Crystal, D., 2003).

The Outer circle included countries that had previously been colonised (invaded) by the English empire such as India, Nigeria, Pakistan, and South Africa. Finally, the Expanding circle included countries that had no official colonial legacy but still used the English language as a secondary language such as China, Japan, Russia and Brazil. The model attempted to illustrate how the English language had different functions and usage depending on the cultural and societal influences.

However, many critics later highlighted that the model oversimplified the sociolinguistic realities, implied a linguistic hierarchy and didn't account for the fluid identity and usage of the English language in the globalised world (Crystal, D., 2003).

Global Language

During the 17th and 18th century the English language began to emerge as the most common language used in science and technology, which assisted in funding, influence and research across cultural barriers, which further assisted in cementing the English language as a primary language, and as a lingua franca, secondary language across the world.

The expansion of schooling in the 18th and 19th centuries institutionalised the English language. Its development was shaped by Curriculum decisions (what English was taught and how), Grammatical instruction based on prescriptive norms and the mass introduction of Testing and assessment, which privileged "standard" English as the "correct and only form". This greatly improved literacy in children and adults, and indirectly improved communication and research (because of the growth in growth of printing, libraries and wider access), however, like many developments discussed throughout this book it did come at a cost. The institutionalising of the English language reinforced social hierarchies (with lower and middle-class children often being seen as less intelligent), language-based discrimination (with regional and class pronunciations being discouraged and punished) and led to further homogenisation (standardisation) of language use (Crystal, D., 2003).

By the 18th century the British empire had a presence across almost 25% of the world, with large companies such as the 'British East India Company' further assisting with this spread of language through trade and other questionable business practices even by the standards of the time. The timing of the spread of the English language, greatly assisted in its spread and ongoing use. Three factors that have been attributed to British English spreading during the 18-20th centuries include physical print media, increased rates of literacy amongst most English-speaking groups and an increase in non-print media such as theatre, cinema, music, radios and later television.

England served different functions in different countries. In Australia and North America, it was used as the primary settler language, whereas in India it was used for administrative purposes such as governing the civil service, conducting legal proceedings, drafting official correspondence, and facilitating communication between British officials and diverse linguistic communities.

As the British empire reduced in influence and power, the English-speaking empire of the United States of America grew in economic, military, political and entertainment power, further enhancing the influence of the English language. During the late 20th century other technological advancements such as the internet and transnational companies cemented the English language as a dominant language worldwide (Crystal, D., 2003).

There are (at the time of writing) an estimated 1.5 billion English speaking people with many variants across the world all influenced by different cultural and societal needs and wants as well as different historical, political and geographic differences. There are over 160 different variants of the English language with more than 130 countries having English as a part of their core curriculum at school and at least another 40 countries offering as optional curriculum. There is no governing body that enforce or concretely explain what standard English is (unlike with French), and this allows for more variations in the language as well as allows for a more natural spread of the English language (Mufwene, S. S., 2015).

The most well documented examples of English language variants and dialects include American English (Southern, Midwestern, AAVE/ African American Vernacular English, Cajun English), Australian English (Standard, Broad, Cultivated, various Indigenous Australian English), Bahamian Creole English, Bangladeshi English, British English (Cockney, Estuary, Scouse), Burmese English, Canadian English (Western, Newfoundland, Maritime), Caribbean English, Dutch English, Fijian English, Finnish English, Gambian English, German English, Ghanaian English, Guyanese English, Hong Kong English, Indian English, Irish English (Hiberno-English), Jamaican English, Kenyan English, Korean English, Liberian English, Mainland Chinese English, Malaysian English, Nepali English, New Zealand English, Nigerian English, Philippine English, Scottish English, Singaporean English, South African English, Sri Lankan English, Swedish English, Tanzanian English, Ugandan English, Welsch English and Zimbabwean English.

Unlike the French language, which is governed by strict rules from the Académie Française, English has developed without a central regulatory body. This means that all variations, despite their differences in pronunciation, grammar, vocabulary and social use, can still be considered a version of English (Mufwene, S. S., 2015).

English is now used as the second language when performing diplomacy or similar political discussions, over taking French in the 20th Century. During the industrial revolution the use of the English language internationally had begun to spread, and this only increased during the first world war, when for the first time, it was formally used to write the negotiated treaties (such as the Treaty of Versailles) alongside French for the first time (Jenkins, J., & Baker, W., 2023).

This helped to concrete the English language as one of the diplomatic languages of the world. Following the outcomes of World War two, France's global influenced had dramatically reduced and instead the United States of America became a global power with their dominant language being English. Due to the USA's economic and military power, the English language quickly spread and with the increased uptake of cinema, music, television and fast food world-wide, the English language spread more quickly, slowly influencing people around the world.

Technology such as computers and emailing only increased and solidified English on the international stage. The first recognisable email was sent in 1971 by Ray Tomlinson, a computer engineer working on ARPANET, a project funded by the U.S. Department of Defence's ARPA (Advanced Research Projects Agency). The invention of the internet led to thousands of new words being invented (Email, Blog, Hashtag, Phishing) and many existing words being repurposed with new digital meanings words being repurposed (Cloud, Mouse, Stream, Virus, Friend, Surf, Wall). Linguists and lexicographers widely agree that the late 20th and early 21st centuries saw the largest explosion of acronyms in English history, driven by digital communication's need for speed, clarity, and space-saving, as users sought to communicate quickly and efficiently in online environments (Jenkins, J., & Baker, W., 2023).

By the early 21st century it was estimated that the modern English language was influenced by over 350 languages from direct and indirect interactions with various cultures and technologies, with some influences being subtle and others more overt (Mufwene, S. S., 2015).

As discussed throughout this book, words' meanings can change over time by broadening, narrowing or flipping. Broadening is when the word goes from a specific meaning such as holiday to mean a religious festival to a broader meaning such as having a planned break. Narrowing is when the words' meaning reduces such as meat referring to food, to now meaning specifically animal flesh.

Flipping includes Pejoration such as silly previously meaning happy or blessed to now meaning foolish, and Amelioration such as Knight going from servant to denoting a noble warrior to now meaning a noble title. Its meaning can also move from the literal to the metaphorical such as "grasping" originally meaning to physically grab something, to it now being used to mean "to understand the idea" (an intellectual grasping) (Jenkins, J., & Baker, W., 2023).

English also has multiple words that mean similar or the same thing because of its complicated history and myriad of influences. Ask comes from Old English, Inquire comes from French and Interrogate comes from Latin. All three words have very similar meanings and highlight the uniqueness and ability of

English to absorb and evolve over time (Jenkins, J., & Baker, W., 2023).

Modern English Nouns, Verbs & More

This section will discuss how the English language is used today. There are many classes and even more subclasses depending on how we choose to define the types of words. The four major word classes include nouns, verbs, adjectives and adverbs.

Other word classes include prepositions, pronouns, determiners, conjunctions, interjections, prefixes, suffixes, tenses, acronyms, paralinguistics, particles, grammatical expletives and neologisms. This section was drawn largely from Huddleston, R., & Pullum, G. (2005) and Crystal, D. (2003) work, but also from various other sources listed in the references section.

4 Major word classes

Nouns

Nouns are words that name people, places things or ideas. Common examples can include dog, teacher, water, table and happiness. Proper nouns are words that name important people or things such as London, Queen Elizabeth and Old English. Nouns originated during the Old English period.

Verbs

Verbs are words that express an action or a state of being. Common examples can include running, thinking, eating, is and grow. There are subtypes of verbs known as Modal verbs and Auxiliary verbs. Modal verbs express necessity, possibility, permission or ability. Common examples can include can, could, may, might, must, shall, should, will and would. Auxiliary verbs are used with the main verbs to form tenses, voices, and moods. Common examples can include be, have and do. Verbs originated during the Old English period.

Adjectives

Adjectives are words that describe or modify nouns. Common examples can include blue, tall, angry, old, fast and young. Adjectives originated during the Old English period.

Adverbs

Adverbs are words that describe or modify verbs. Common examples can include quickly, very, silently, now, here and high. Intensifiers are adverbs that amplify or reduce intensity such as very, so, too, incredibly and extremely. Adverbs originated during the Old English period.

Other word classes

Prepositions

Prepositions are words that show the relationship between a noun or pronoun and another word in the sentence. Common examples can include on, under, between, during and through. Prepositions originated during the Old English period.

Pronouns

Pronouns are words that replace nouns to avoid repetition when naming. They can be neutral such as it, they, this, who and ourselves; or they can have a gendered tone added such he, she, his and hers. Pronouns originated during the Old English period.

Determiners

Determiners are words that are placed in front of nouns to clarify what the noun refers to. Common examples can include the, a, an, some, many, my, each, his and hers. Determiners originated during the Old English period, with adaptations occurring during Modern English.

Conjunctions

Conjunctions are words that link words, phrases or clauses. Common examples can include and, but, or, although and because. Conjunctions originated during the Old English period.

Interjections

Interjections are words or phrases that express strong emotion or sudden feeling. Common examples can include wow, oh, ouch and yikes. Interjections originated during the Old English period.

Prefixes

Prefixes are word parts that are added at the beginning of a root word to change its meaning. Common examples can include un (unhelpful), re (redo) or dis (disorganised). Prefixes were adapted during the Old English period.

Suffixes

Suffixes are word parts that are added at the end of a root word to form a new word or change its grammatical function. Common examples can include ing (jumping), ly (quickly), ness (kindness), and ed (walked). Suffixes were adapted during the Old English period.

Tenses

Tense refers to the time of action or state expressed, often by the verb. The English language has a complex system when using tenses. The three most common types include Present Simple tense (She walks), Past Simple tense (She walked) and Future Simple tense (She will walk). Present and Past Simple tense originated during Old English whilst Future Simple tense originated during Middle English and Early Modern English. The other types of tenses include: Present Continuous tense (She is walking – Early Modern English), Past Continuous tense (She was walking – Early Modern English), Future Continuous (She will be walking – Early Modern to Modern English), Present Perfect tense (She has walked – Late Middle – Early Modern English), Past Perfect tense (She had walked – Early Modern English), Future Perfect tense (She will have walked – Modern English), Present Perfect Continuous tense (She has been walking – Modern English), Past Perfect Continuous (She had been walking – Modern English) and Future Perfect Continuous (She will have been walking – Modern English).

Acronyms

Acronyms are abbreviations formed from the initial letters of words and pronounced as words such as NATO (North Atlantic Treaty Organisation) and SCUBA (Self-Contained Underwater Breathing Apparatus) or as individual letters such as BBC (British Broadcasting Corporation). Acronyms are considered to be a Modern English development, potentially developing following the growth of bureaucracy, military, science and technology in the later twentieth century. The use of acronyms increased exponentially since digital technology and internet culture became part of our daily lives.

Paralinguistics

Paralinguistics are the non-verbal aspects of communication that accompany speech and affect meaning. They can include tone of voice, facial expressions, gestures, clicks (tsk tsk), posture, pauses, volume and pitch, eye contact and various other body language positions. Paralinguistics are thought to have always existed and adapted during all development of language.

Particles

Particles are small words that don't neatly fit into other word classes. Common examples include up (give up) and off (take off). Particles originated during the Old English period and adapted during Modern English.

Grammatical Expletives

Grammatical Expletives are the words that serve a structural purpose but do not carry their own meaning. Common examples include It (It is raining) and There (There is a book on the table).

Grammatical Expletives originated during the Old English period and adapted across all of English development.

Neologisms and Functional Shifts

These are words that shift class without changing form. Common examples include Google (shifting from noun to verb), Text (shift from noun to verb) and Adult (shifting from noun to adjective). These have become much more common since the digital era of technology.

Pronunciation & Basic Rules in Modern English

It is estimated that 32 percent of Modern English comes from "native" Old English, 45% from French, 17% from Latin, 4% from other Germanic influences and 2% of unknown origins. Today, native English speakers are thought to have a vocabulary of 40000-60000 words. Knowing words is only the start because you can't speak a language without having at least a basic understanding of how to use the words. It is thought that 'Grammar' generates a language through the structure of the sounds (known as phonetics and phonology), the words (morphology), the sentence structure (syntax), the rules for understanding the meaning (semantics) and how "appropriate use" is defined (pragmatics) (Baugh, A., C., & Cable, T., 2002).

Despite officially only having 5 vowels in the alphabet, Modern English has closer to 13 vowels in practice as can be seen by the following words – bit, beet, bait, bet, bat, but, bye, boy, boat, boot, bout, bath and bore. English has no an added tone with the pronunciation unlike the Chinese dialects and Navajo language and no nasalised or lengthened vowels like the Navajo. Officially the English alphabet has 21 consonants, but again in practice there are at least 25 consonants including combining letters such as th, and ch.

One of the key functions of language is to indicate who does what to whom and where, when, how and why this occurs. Modern English makes use of prepositions and strict word order to assist in understanding the grammatical roles of nouns and verbs, compensating for the loss of the case endings and inflectional markers that were present in earlier forms of the language, such as Old English. It was a change from synthetic to analytic use of language. Within a language, exists varieties which can be cultural, geographical, formal (diplomacy), industry (jargon) and even social (class) based. Standard language is the agreed upon use of language from one social group to the rest, often witnessed by what is taught in school.

Two major types of change can occur regarding language change, external and internal. External change can be caused by – interaction between speakers of different languages, innovations by speakers (often by influential people), issues involving political, social, cultural or religious identity, geography (oceans spreading language and mountain ranges isolating pockets of people), migration, trends (financial, fashion, cultural), and more direct often less positive changes such as war, invasion and slavery.

Internal changes can be caused by – speakers slowly adopting the use of words instead of inflections (of, for, have), children hearing the words slightly differently and therefore changing pronunciations and grammar use, the meaning of the word changing to fit a different context (time, location), or the category of the word changing (prepositions being used to introduce sentences).

One tool used to reduce internal change is known as Prescriptive Rules. These are often explicitly taught in education settings where specific language structures and rules are taught and assessed (often with the standard or formal use of the language being encouraged or enforced and alterations being discouraged or punished). Regarding external change, it is often difficult to restrict this as it happens fluidly, multi-directionally, and has too many variables to control; with the English language having no official governing body (unlike the French language governing body the 'French Academy'), new words are added frequently. As is the case in nature, language changes rarely occur as either internal or external, with both influencing each other. These changes rarely occur quickly and this is easily represented by the English language differences between Old English, Middle English, Early Modern English and Modern English (Baugh, A., C., & Cable, T., 2002).

The 2006 OED lists over 23 different spellings throughout history for the word shirt. Most phonetic variation in the English language occurs in vowels with words such as pin and pen, Mary and marry sounding very similar for some variations. Consonant spelling also changes with the k sound of keep spelled ck after short vowels (lack, sick, Rick, deck), k after long vowels (week, soak, shake) and before front vowels (keep, kin, kettle), and c before back vowels (cool, could, cold, cup). The same k sound is spelled differently in borrowed words such as psychology and choral (Crystal, D., 2014).

Loan words confuse English language pronunciation, where some words have had attempts to convert them into English while other words have no such attempt and instead the speaker attempts to focus on the original pronunciation (such as French or Latin). Examples of loan words include Phoenix, suite, xylophone, quota, gnomic, euphemism, debris and glacier (de Heer, M., Blokland, R., Dunn, M., & Vesakoski, O., 2024).

Modern English vowels can be described using three tongue positions: firstly, whether the tongue is high or low, secondly whether the tongue is front or back, and lastly, the duration of the sound. High Vowels (Tongue is high in the mouth) examples include Front High ("ee" as in beet, and "i" as in bit) and Back High ("oo" as in boot).

Mid Vowels (Tongue is in the middle height) examples include Front Mid ("ay" as in bait, and "e" as in bet), Central Mid ("uh" as in the unstressed part of sofa, and "u" as in but) and Back Mid Vowels ("oh" as in boat, "aw" as in bought, and "oy" as in boy).

Low Vowels (Tongue is low in the mouth) examples include Front Low ("a" as in bat) and Central Low ("ah" as in father). There is also a changing position of the tongue known as Diphthongs (where vowel combinations slide from one sound to another) including "eye" as in bite and "ow" as in bout (Crystal, D., 2018).

The Great Vowel Shift affected primarily long vowels which is evidenced in English pairs such as sane/sanity, vain/vanity, grain/granary, humane/humanity, clean/cleanliness, malign/malignant, crime/criminal and sign/signify.

Vowels let air flow freely, but consonants block air at certain spots in the mouth known as places of articulation. For example, (p) and (b) use the lips, while (th) sounds like in "thin" or "this" use the tongue and teeth. Air may be fully or partly blocked, like how (p) blocks fully, and (f) only partly. All vowels use the voice, but not all consonants do. There are three main features that define consonants: how the air is blocked (manner), where it's blocked (place), and if the voice is used (voicing).

Some consonant sounds stop air completely (like p, b, t, d, k, g) and are called stops. Others let air pass with friction (like f, v, s, z) and are called fricatives. Some mix both, like ch and j sounds and are called affricates. Nasals and Liquids have a lot in common with vowels as they can be syllables on their own. Nasals let air out through the nose (like m, n), and Liquids, like l and r, use the voice and vary across languages. Glides, like w and y, are like vowels and go with them in speech. Places of articulation include the Lips (p, b, m, f, v), Teeth (th) sounds, the Ridge behind upper teeth (alveolar) (t, d, n, s, z, l, r), the front of the palate (alveo-palatal) (sh, ch, j), the Palate (y), the Back of the palate (velar) (k, g, ng), and the Throat (glottal) (h) (Crystal, D., 2018).

Most consonants come in pairs of a voiced and a voiceless sound. Voiced sounds are made when the vocal folds in the larynx vibrate. For example, (f) and (s) are voiceless, and (v) and (z) are voiced.

In English, words can be formed by means of prefixes, such as pre- and anti-, or suffixes, such as -ness and the plural -s. These word-building rules have not changed much in character since Old English and involve derivational prefixes and suffixes. There are also other ways to construct new words, such as compounding and shortening. Examples include "notebook" (compound of note + book), "sunflower", and shortened forms like "ad" (from advertisement) or "phone" (from telephone).

Words can also be marked as being the subject or object of a sentence, for plural and possession by means of inflectional markers, more commonly known as grammatical endings. Common examples in English include the plural -s (as in cats), the possessive 's (as in the girl's book), and the past tense -ed (as in walked).

It is more common, however, for Modern English nouns and verbs not to be marked for case and agreement, but the word order has to be strictly observed. Common examples in English include "The dog chased the cat" versus "The cat chased the dog", where reversing the word order completely changes the meaning. Similarly, "She is singing" (subject–verb–continuous action) differs in meaning from "Is she singing?" (inverted for a question) (Crystal, D., 2018).

Currently in education systems across Australia the American English and the British English have become confused regarding specific writing rules. For example, currently a percentage of schools in Australia are teaching the American use of inverter commas in primary school .

In traditional Modern English, the use of inverter commas had slight difference in American English compared to British English. For example, the American English would write the sentence as Bob said "the cat is on the mat." However, British English would write the same sentence as Bob said "the cat is on the mat" (Crystal, D., 2018).

In Australian English the written rules that had been established have begun to change depending on the teacher and education institution. Other examples of Australian English following British English rules less and following American English rules more include – the use of the past simple instead of present perfect, such as I already ate (American) instead of I have already eaten (British), double quotation marks as default, e.g. "Hello" (American) instead of 'Hello' (British), and the Comma before the final item in a list (Oxford comma), which is more common in American English: apples, bananas, and oranges.

Despite my best efforts to follow the British English rules while writing this book, I too have fluctuated between American and British English rules. This is perhaps a natural example of regional difference or perhaps an example of the natural evolution of written English language changes.

Homophones (words that sound the same but are different in meaning or spelling) arose because of changes in pronunciation over time, particularly during the Great Vowel Shift, where different words with distinct historical spellings and meanings converged phonetically. Today many homophones remain, which simultaneously adds to the richness of the Modern English language but also creates potential for ambiguity, misunderstandings, and puns.

Homographs (words that are spelled the same but differ in meaning or pronunciation) also remain in the English language because English has absorbed vocabulary from many languages and historical stages without always changing spelling to match evolving pronunciation, allowing multiple meanings to attach to the same written form (Crystal, D., 2018).

Informal communication in Modern English has introduced ideas such as the Quotative "Be like". Today it is used to introduce reported speech, thought or internal reaction instead of using the traditional structure of using verbs to introduce the speech, thought or internal. An example of the difference is using the phrase "I was like" instead of saying "I asked". The quotative "Be like" includes a form of the verb "to be" followed by "like" and a quote. In current Modern English it is also used to convey attitude, emotion or a stance. The use and meaning is often performative or illustrative rather than just descriptive. Its use began as a preposition (She looks like her mother), then became a discourse marker (like you know what I mean) and finally morphed into how we use it today (Tagliamonte, S., & Roberts, C., 2005).

The other recent evolution in Modern English for its use in informal communication is the "Get" passive. It is used to replace the traditional verb such as "He got fired" instead of the traditional use "He was fired". Unlike the "Be like" which focuses on drama and expression, the "Get" passive, is used to emphasise agency or unexpectedness "She got scratched by a cat" sounds more urgent then "She was scratched".

The "Get" passive also emphasises involvement or responsibility ("She got arrested" suggests partial fault or misfortune) and resultative aspects (focuses on the result and not the process). Its use became increasingly popular during the late 20th century but has been found in late 17th century texts Tagliamonte, S., & Roberts, C., 2005).

Concluding – English the Ever-Changing Language

The history of the English language is a testament to our ability to adapt, absorb, and create. Over a period of more than fifteen centuries, it has transformed from a cluster of West Germanic dialects spoken by settlers on the British Isles into a global lingua franca used in politics, science, business, media, and everyday conversation. The journey from Old English to Modern English is not one of linear progress, but of continual reshaping, forged by contact, conflict, commerce, creativity, cultural exchange, change, character and technology.

The English language's earliest recorded stage, Old English, was an unmistakable mix of its Germanic roots. Inflectional endings conveyed grammatical information, word order was relatively free, and vocabulary reflected both the native Anglo-Saxon world and the borrowings of earlier contact with Celtic speakers and Latin-speaking Romans. This early period already showed the adaptive nature of English. While firmly Germanic in structure, Old English incorporated loan words for new concepts, religious terms from Latin, placenames from Celtic, and practical vocabulary from Norse neighbours.

It was a language of oral tradition, only gradually moving into manuscript form with the arrival of Christian scribes. Poetry relied on alliteration and formulaic phrasing, and prose served law, religion, and administration. The Viking invasions of the 8th–11th centuries introduced Old Norse words and, crucially, nudged English grammar toward simplification by eroding inflectional endings and promoting a more fixed word order.

The Norman Conquest of 1066 marked a dramatic turning point. For over three centuries, English existed alongside Norman French and Latin in a multilingual environment. French dominated the law, government, aristocracy and in a different way food, Latin remained the language of the church, and English continued as the tongue of the common people.

Spelling and pronunciation began to shift under French scribal influence: *cw* became *qu* (*queen*), *hus* became *house*, runic letters like thorn (þ) gave way to digraphs (*th*), and *uu* evolved into *w*. These orthographic changes both reflected and reinforced phonological developments already underway.

Middle English also saw greater dialect diversity, as regional variations in pronunciation, vocabulary, and grammar flourished without a central authority to enforce standardisation. Literary works like Chaucer's Canterbury Tales not only captured the richness of these varieties but also showcased the growing potential of English for complex narrative, satire, and poetic artistry.

The transition to Early Modern English, from roughly 1500 to 1700, was shaped by several intertwined forces: the Renaissance, the printing press, exploration, and the beginnings of British colonial expansion. The Great Vowel Shift, a major phonological reorganisation, radically altered the sound system, setting Modern English pronunciation apart from its medieval ancestors while leaving much of the spelling unchanged. This mismatch between orthography and pronunciation remains one of English's defining quirks.

The printing press, introduced to England by William Caxton in 1476, catalysed standardisation in spelling and grammar, although "standard" in this period still meant considerable variation. With print came the mass production of books, pamphlets, and eventually newspapers, allowing ideas to circulate more quickly and widely than ever before. Writers like Shakespeare, and purposeful translations such as the King James' Bible, expanded the lexicon through invention, adaptation, and creative recombination, leaving a permanent mark on the idioms and metaphors we still use today.

The global voyages of the Elizabethan and Jacobean periods brought English into contact with a widening array of languages. Borrowings from Spanish, Portuguese, Dutch, and indigenous languages of the Americas, Africa, and Asia entered the vocabulary, often alongside the goods, concepts, and cultural practices they named.

From the 18th century onward, the pace of change accelerated. Dictionaries by Samuel Johnson and others sought to fix spelling and meaning, but expansion was inevitable. The Industrial Revolution introduced new technical vocabulary, the rise of Britain as a colonial power embedded English in regions across the globe, where it mingled with local languages to produce new varieties and creoles.

American English, diverging in spelling, pronunciation, and idiom, grew in influence through its literature, newspapers, and later its dominance in film, radio, and television. Technological advances from the telegraph to the telephone introduced new words (telegram, long-distance) and new styles of brevity, anticipating the clipped, efficient forms of digital communication today.

In Australia, Canada, New Zealand, India, and other regions, English evolved in dialogue with local languages and cultures, producing distinctive vocabularies and idioms that now form part of the global English mosaic. The resulting linguistic diversity is both a challenge for standardisation and a strength, providing endless resources for creativity and adaptation.

English today is spoken by more people, in more contexts, than at any other point in its history. Its vocabulary spans the practical and the poetic, the ancient and the cutting-edge. It carries the weight of its history from Beowulf to the Beatles, from Chaucer to chatbots and it continues to remain a language in motion.

The story of English is, ultimately, the story of its speakers: their migrations, conquests, innovations, and imaginations. Every borrowed word, every grammatical shift, every new expression reflects a human choice to adapt language to the needs of the moment. That is why English has survived, thrived, and spread: it bends without breaking, changes without losing its core, and expands without rejecting its past.

As we move deeper into the 21st century, English will continue to be shaped by forces both familiar and unprecedented. The same currents of contact, creativity, and technology that carried it from the mead halls of Anglo-Saxon England to the screens of the digital age will carry it onward. Its history is not a closed book, but an open conversation, one in which every speaker, writer, and reader plays a part.

Will the English language continue to thrive and adapt or will the global world we live in allow for another language to become the new lingua franca in the near future?

References

Balliet, G. (2013). Railroads and their Effect on American Society, 1840-1890. Saber and Scroll, 2(4), 4.

Baugh, A., C., & Cable, T. (2002). *A History of the English Language: Fifth Edition*. Routledge, Taylor and Francis Group.

Bennett, Ľ. L., Harišová, K., Formánková, A., & Joukl, Z. (2025). *From hieroglyphs to emoji: a spiral model for writing systems evolution*. Semiotica.

Berensmeyer, I. (2020). *A short media history of English*. Cambridge University Press.

Blackmore, S. (1999). The Meme Machine. Oxford University Press, Oxford.

Blake, N., & Hogg, R. M. (Eds.). (1992). *The Cambridge history of the English language* (Vol. 1). Cambridge University Press.

Brozovsky, E., Hinrichs, L., Ahlers, W., Bergs, A., Bohmann, A., Meemann, K., & Schultz, P. (2016, February). *Sibilants and ethnic diversity: A sociophonetic study of palatalized /s/ in STR clusters among Hispanic, White, and African-American speakers of Texas English* [Conference presentation]. 16th Texas Linguistics Society Conference, University of Texas at Austin, Austin, TX, United States.

Burchfield, R. (Ed.). (1994). The Cambridge history of the English language. Volume V: English in Britain and overseas: Origins and development. Cambridge University Press

Camlot, J. (2019). *Phonopoetics: The Making of Early Literary Recordings*. Stanford University Press.

Chandra, P., & Verma, P. (2024). *The English Language: Transformations Through the Ages.*

Clark, S. (1999). *Thinking with demons: the idea of witchcraft in early modern Europe.* Oxford University Press.

Chomsky, N. (1965). *Aspects of the Theory of Syntax.*

Crystal, B., & Crystal, D. (2004). *Shakespeare's words: a glossary and language companion.* Penguin UK.

Crystal, D. (2018). *The Cambridge encyclopedia of the English language.* Cambridge university press.

Crystal, D. (2014). *Words in time and place: Exploring language through the historical thesaurus of the Oxford English Dictionary.* Oxford University Press.

Crystal, D. (2003). *English as a global language.* Cambridge university press.

Curtis, T. A. (2024). *Greek and Latin roots of medical and scientific terminologies.* John Wiley & Sons.

Curzan, A. (2003). *Gender shifts in the history of English.* Cambridge University Press.

Daniell, D. (2001). *William Tyndale: a biography.* Yale University Press.

Daniels, P. T. (2013). The history of writing as a history of linguistics. *The Oxford handbook of the history of linguistics, 53-69.*

de Heer, M., Blokland, R., Dunn, M., & Vesakoski, O. (2024). Loanwords in basic vocabulary as an indicator of borrowing profiles. *Journal of Language Contact, 16*(1), 54-103.

Decker, D., & Sumanasekara, S. (2025). *The Origin Of The Eneglish Langauge: A Historical And Linguistic Review.* EPRA International Journal of Research and Development

Djouhaina, C. (2022). Describing the Role of English as a Lingua Franca in Facilitating Intercultural Communication in the Tourism Industry The case of the Travel Agencies in Biskra.

Doten-Snitker, K., Pfaff, S., & Hsiao, Y. (2024). Ideational diffusion and the great witch hunt in Central Europe. *Theory and Society*, *53*(6), 1291-1319.

Farrokhi, F., Ansarin, A. A., & Ashrafi, S. (2019). The conceptual metaphors of building and construction in newspaper and research article. *International Journal of Linguistics, Literature and Translation*, *2*(4), 290328.

Garner, B. A. (2011). *Garner's dictionary of legal usage*. Oxford University Press.

Gelderen, E. (2006). *A History of the English Language*. John Benjamins Publishing Company.

Georgieva, V. (2015). Military English: From theory to practice.

Godden, M., & Lapidge, M. (Eds.). (2013). *The Cambridge companion to old English literature*. Cambridge University Press.

Greiffenstern, S. (2010). *The influence of computers, the internet and computer-mediated communication on everyday English*. Logos Verlag Berlin GmbH.

Hanlon, W. W., Heblich, S., Monte, F., & Schmitz, M. B. (2022). *A penny for your thoughts* (No. w30076). National Bureau of Economic Research.

Hejná, M., & Walkden, G. (2021). *The history of English.* Language Science Press.

Hofrichter, F. F., & Yoshimoto, M. (Eds.). (2021). *Women, Aging, and Art: A Crosscultural Anthology.* Bloomsbury Publishing USA.

Hogg, R. M. (Ed.). (1992). The Cambridge history of the English language. Volume I: The beginnings to 1066. Cambridge University Press.

Horáková, J., & Kelemen, J. (2008). 12 The Robot Story: Why Robots Were Born and How They Grew Up.

Huddleston, R., & Pullum, G. (2005). The Cambridge grammar of the English language. *Zeitschrift für Anglistik und Amerikanistik, 53*(2), 193-194.

Jenkins, J., & Baker, W. (2023). *English as a Lingua Franca.* In *Oxford Bibliographies.* Oxford University Press.

Johnson, K. (2024). *Landmarks in the History of the English Language.* Routledge.

Jones, W. (1786). *The Third Anniversary Discourse, on the Hindus* (in *The Works of Sir William Jones*, ed. Lord Teignmouth). Cambridge University Press.

Leith, D., & Graddol, D., with contributions by Jackson, L. (2006). Modernity and English as a national language. In D. Graddol, D. Leith, J. Swann, M. Rhys, & J. Gillen (Eds.), Changing English (pp. 79–112). Routledge.

Lerer, S. (2008). *The history of the English language* (2nd ed.). The Teaching Company.

Maci, S., Demata, M., McGlashan, M., & Seargeant, P. (Eds.). (2024). *The Routledge handbook of discourse and disinformation*. Routledge.

McIntosh, A., Samuels, M. L., Benskin, M., Laing, M., & Williamson, K. (1986). *A linguistic atlas of late mediaeval English*. Aberdeen University Press.

McKitterick, D. (2003). Print, manuscript and the search for order, 1450-1830. Cambridge University Press

Milne, G. J. (2007). British business and the telephone, 1878–1911. *Business History*, *49*(2), 163-185.

Miyagawa, S., Lesure, C., & Nóbrega, V. A. (2018). Cross-modality information transfer: A hypothesis about the relationship among prehistoric cave paintings, symbolic thinking, and the emergence of language. *Frontiers in Psychology*, *9*, 115.

Mufwene, S. S. (2015). Colonization, indigenization, and the differential evolution of English: Some ecological perspectives. *World Englishes*, *34*(1), 6-21.

Nunberg, G. (2001). *The Way We Talk Now: Commentaries on Language and Culture from NPR's" Fresh Air"*. Houghton Mifflin Harcourt.

Pascali, L. (2017). The wind of change: Maritime technology, trade, and economic development. *American Economic Review*, *107*(9), 2821-2854.

Perkin, H. (2003). *The origins of modern English society*. Routledge.

Peterson, D. J. (2015). *The art of language invention: From horse-lords to dark elves to sand worms, the words behind world-building*. Penguin.

Radul, S., & Kharlamova, L. (2023). ICAO phonetic alphabet evolution.

Read, A. W. (1978). The sources of ghost words in English. *Word, 29*(2), 95-104.

Richards, O. (2018). Short stories in English for beginners. Teach Yourself

Ringe, D. (2017). *From Proto-Indo-European to Proto-Germanic* (Vol. 1). Oxford University Press.

Rissanen, M., & Lass, R. (1999). The Cambridge history of the English language.

Rodríguez Gil, M. E. (2002). Ann Fisher: first female grammarian. *Historical Sociolinguistics and Sociohistorical Linguistics*.

Rogers, S. D. (2015). Invented Languages of Fantasy and Science Fiction: A Dynamic Writing System for a Speakerless People. *Journal of Language Creation, 3*(2), 5–27.

Romaine, S. (Ed.). (1999). The Cambridge history of the English language. Volume IV: 1776–1997. Cambridge University Press.

Rosenfelder, M. (2009). *The Language Construction Kit*. CreateSpace.

Saag, L., Laneman, M., Varul, L., Malve, M., Valk, H., et. al. (2019). *The arrival of Siberian ancestry connecting the Eastern Baltic to Uralic speakers further east*. Current Biology, 29(10), 1701–1711.e16.

Saguy, A. C., & Williams, J. A. (2022). A little word that means a lot: A reassessment of singular they in a new era of gender politics. *Gender & Society*, *36*(1), 5-31.

Salo, D. (2004). *A Gateway to Sindarin: A grammar of an Elvish language from JRR Tolkien's Lord of the Rings*. University of Utah Press.

Sanleandro, M. P. (2015). A Study of Nautical Terms and Their Use in Everyday Language.

Schneiderová, A. (2018). Historical background to English legal language. *Journal of Modern Science*, *37*(2), 117-126.

Schreiber, L. (2005). The importance of precision in language: Communication research and (so-called) alternative medicine. *Health Communication*, *17*(2), 173-190.

Sharpe, J. (2019). *Witchcraft in early modern England*. Routledge.

Smith, G., Fleisig, E., Bossi, M., Rustagi, I., & Yin, X. (2024). Standard language ideology in ai-generated language. *arXiv preprint arXiv:2406.08726*.

Smith, J. J. (2006). *From middle to early modern English* (pp. 120-146). Oxford University Press.

Sundberg, M. (2015). *Old World language families* [Illustration]. Vivid Maps.

Sylvia IV, J. J. (2024). Introduction to Communication and Media Studies.

Tagliamonte, S., & Roberts, C. (2005). So weird; so cool; so innovative: The use of intensifiers in the television series Friends. *American speech*, *80*(3), 280-300.

Trenité, G. N. (1870–1946). *The Chaos* poem. In C. Upward (Ed.), The Classic Concordance of Cacographic Chaos (*Journal of the Simplified Spelling Society*, 17, 1994/2, pp. 27–32). Manchester: The Simplified Spelling Society

Tonkin, H. (2015). Introduction: In Search of Esperanto. *Interdisciplinary Description of Complex Systems: INDECS, 13*(2), 182-192.

Wallage, P. W. (2017). *Negation in early English: Grammatical and functional change*. Cambridge University Press.

Wang, Y. (2023). Poetics of the Medial State of Emily Dickinson's Persona. *Journal of Literary Studies, 39*(1), 1-14.

Wells, J. C. (1982). *Accents of english* (Vol. 3, pp. 99-100). Cambridge: Cambridge University Press.

Wells, John C. (2000). Longman Pronunciation Dictionary. Harlow, England Pearson Education Ltd.

Wodak, R., & Forchtner, B. (Eds.). (2018). *The Routledge handbook of language and politics* (pp. 572-586). London and New York: Routledge.

Wolfe, P. M. (1972). *Linguistic change and the great vowel shift in English*. Univ of California Press.

Yule, G. (2022). *The study of language*. Cambridge university press.

Index

Adverbs, 91, 122, 166, 168
Aitchinson, 57
Alliteration, 86, 188
Artificial Intelligence, 69
Atkins, 57
Auxiliaries, 106, 107, 121, 122, 123
Aviation, 62, 68
Bunyan, 123
Business, 36, 37, 38, 46, 66, 69, 79, 159, 187, 197
Caxton, 189
Celtic, 10, 19, 20, 74, 76, 78, 187
Chaucer, 43, 99, 100, 106, 139, 189, 191
Columbus, 150
Commerce, 38, 39, 187
Comparative Philology, 6
Computer, 163, 195
Computing, 52, 65
Conjunctions, 92, 166
Construction, 27, 68, 195
Crystal, 22, 32, 33, 36, 42, 43, 51, 58, 135, 137, 149, 152, 156, 157, 159, 160, 166, 178, 180, 181, 182, 183, 184, 194
Dent, 58
Determiners, 83, 122, 138, 166
Dialects, 10, 20, 48, 58, 70, 88, 98, 117, 118, 161, 175, 187
Early Modern English, 30, 101, 108, 116, 117, 119, 120, 121, 122, 123, 138, 171, 178, 189
Entertainment, 30, 31, 160
Fashion, 67, 177
Food, 12, 39, 79, 149, 150, 151, 162, 164, 188

French, 10, 20, 53, 55, 57, 60, 64, 77, 79, 80, 81, 84, 89, 97, 99, 100, 101, 102, 103, 106, 109, 118, 119, 120, 136, 138, 150, 160, 161, 162, 164, 175, 178, 179, 188
Gaelic, 10, 20, 74
Gender, 56, 83, 87, 88, 89, 115, 138, 139, 140, 141, 199
Germanic, 9, 10, 18, 19, 21, 23, 49, 74, 76, 77, 85, 86, 90, 92, 96, 119, 127, 128, 129, 131, 138, 175, 187, 198
Global, 9, 23, 24, 31, 38, 39, 46, 50, 62, 63, 64, 65, 155, 162, 187, 190, 191, 192, 194
Great Vowel Shift, 94, 96, 102, 114, 119, 124, 125, 127, 180, 184, 189
Greek, 10, 17, 21, 54, 56, 60, 127, 130, 136, 144, 145, 194
Homographs, 184
Homophones, 184
Indo-European, 9, 17, 18, 21, 49, 90, 127, 128, 129, 131, 149, 198
Inflection, 83, 87
Inflectional, 22, 79, 83, 84, 138, 176, 182, 188
Inflections, 84, 87, 94, 119, 177
Interjections, 170
Irish, 20, 50, 74, 83, 161
Jargon, 37, 60, 63, 64, 65, 67, 176
Jonson, 123
Late Modern English, 115
Latin, 10, 17, 21, 52, 53, 54, 55, 56, 60, 74, 75, 77, 78, 79, 81, 83, 97, 101, 109, 119, 127, 130, 133, 136, 139, 144, 145, 146, 164, 175, 179, 187, 188, 194
Lingua Franca, 9, 23, 24, 158, 187, 192
Manuscript, 75, 188
Manuscripts, 83, 114
Medical, 60, 82, 194

Middle English, 23, 25, 53, 54, 79, 84, 93, 94, 98, 100, 101, 102, 103, 104, 105, 106, 107, 108, 110, 111, 112, 113, 114, 116, 117, 118, 119, 122, 123, 124, 131, 136, 138, 171, 178, 189
Military, 63, 64, 65, 75, 78, 160, 162, 172
Modern English, 22, 23, 59, 60, 69, 83, 84, 85, 87, 88, 89, 92, 93, 102, 103, 104, 106, 107, 114, 115, 116, 117, 119, 121, 122, 125, 131, 132, 136, 146, 155, 166, 169, 171, 172, 173, 175, 176, 178, 179, 182, 183, 184, 185, 187, 189
Murray, 44, 57, 140
Music, 27, 30, 39, 69, 82, 159, 162
Norman, 10, 23, 39, 60, 79, 80, 84, 97, 138, 188
OED, 109, 114, 147, 178
Old English, 10, 17, 22, 47, 53, 72, 74, 75, 76, 78, 79, 82, 83, 84, 85, 86, 87, 88, 89, 90, 91, 92, 93, 94, 103, 104, 105, 106, 107, 108, 112, 128, 131, 136, 138, 164, 167, 168, 169, 170, 171, 173, 174, 175, 176, 178, 181, 187
Oral, 17, 75, 188
Parataxis, 92
Prefixes, 45, 78, 93, 112, 166, 181
Printing Press, 26, 27, 28, 126, 133, 135, 143, 145
Pronouns, 83, 87, 88, 89, 91, 92, 103, 104, 110, 112, 119, 120, 140, 141, 166
Regional, 58, 70, 98, 99, 112, 159, 183, 189
Restoration, 114
Sailing, 59
Shakespeare, 42, 45, 53, 120, 139, 146, 147, 190, 194
Shakespeare's, 147
Sociolinguistics, 6, 198
Sports, 66
Standardisation, 32, 99, 143, 144, 147, 153, 159, 189, 191

Suffixes, 45, 93, 166, 181
Sweet, 57
Tenses, 166, 167, 171
Tyndale, 25, 26, 54, 145, 194
Venery, 149
Verbs, 21, 45, 84, 87, 91, 94, 106, 119, 121, 122, 133, 166, 167, 168, 176, 182, 184
Welsh, 47, 74

www.ingramcontent.com/pod-product-compliance
Lightning Source LLC
Chambersburg PA
CBHW071238070526
44583CB00017B/2243